TEACHING

AMERICAN VOICES

MULTICULTURAL LITERACY AND CRITICAL THINKING

Second Edition

INSTRUCTOR'S MANUAL BY DOLORES LAGUARDIA AND HANS P. GUTH

Contributing Manual Author: KAREN HARRINGTON

Mayfield Publishing Company
Mountain View, California
London • Toronto

International Standard Book Number: 1-55934-487-3

Manufactured in the United States of America.

Mayfield Publishing Company
1280 Villa Street
Mountain View, CA 94041

ABOUT THIS MANUAL

This manual is intended as a teacher's resource kit. It provides handy overviews, quick reminders, and sample answers to the questions asked in the text. The aim is to help teachers encourage responsive reading, stimulate class discussion, and guide student writing. We hope instructors will find the material included here useful when trying to help students to get "inside" a selection, to become involved in the issues, or to respond to the eloquence of a committed writer. Some recurrent features:

CHAPTER OVERVIEWS   Brief chapter introductions explain the focus of each chapter and the connecting thread between the readings. These introductions will often spell out the link between the thematic focus or the central issues and the writing or thinking strategies that play a major role in a chapter.

SELECTION HEADNOTES   Brief introductory notes provide the instructor with additional background or a "way in" for a selection.

CLOSE READING   Sample answers enable the instructor to take the student back to the reading for a closer look. They pull out striking details, key metaphors, or revealing quotations. They help the instructor to trace the way an essay takes shape or to chart the flow of an argument. They will often clarify key terms, explain allusions, or provide context.

THE RANGE OF RESPONSE   Responses to questions are meant to be suggestive rather than definitive. The questions in the student text are meant to be open questions, and the sample answers in this manual will often try to suggest the range of pro and con. They will help the teacher validate a range of student responses. There is no attempt here to legislate a single correct answer for some of the complex issues raised in the readings in the text.

THE INTERACTIVE CLASSROOM   The manual will often provide pointers for student work. It will suggest a possible focus, possible issues, or a possible procedure for class activities, group projects, or student writing.

OPTIONAL WORK WITH LANGUAGE   Many teachers will be working with students with limited vocabularies or limited reading range and with others who speak English as a second language. For selected readings, the manual provides samples of language work or dictionary work—often focused on such topics as synonyms, connotation, words' roots, formal and informal language.

CONTENTS

CHAPTER 1

INITIATION: Growing Up American   31

How do we give students early in a course a sense of the challenges and the power of the written word? Why do writers write? What does writing do for the writer, and what does it do for the reader? One way is to start with readings and writing assignments that stay close to the writers' own lives. Writing is a means of recording and illuminating personal experience. Students may not be experts on the legal history of abortion or on the pros and cons of censorship, but they are the authority on what has happened to them in their own lives and what has made them who and what they are. Writing with an autobiographical focus helps them discover writing as a way of exploring, interpreting, and coming to terms with experience.

The readings in this chapter focus on an archetypal American theme: Americans do not grow up in a monolithic culture that tells everyone where and how to live, what to think, and how to worship God. Instead, many young Americans learn to chart their own course between diverse influences and traditions. They navigate between the influence of home and school, or between a family's values and the standards of their peers. They work out their own way of relating to the culture of immigrant parents and the loud "now" culture of mainstream America. The readings in this chapter often focus on a crucial stage in the growing up of a young American. They include the stories of

- a Native American woman in search of the lost or suppressed culture of her people;
- a young African American woman leaving the South and breaking through the barriers of prejudice and job discrimination;
- a boy from a strict religious background rebelling against being "different";
- a daughter discovering the downside of the father's involvement in the jazz culture and the drug scene;
- the child of migrant workers discovering the life of itinerant fruit-pickers following the crops;
- a Chinese American high school student coping with ridicule and gangs;
- a Japanese American poet remembering a father marked by life in the relocation camps.

Mary Crow Dog, "Lakota Woman"   33

One reviewer called Mary Crow Dog's book "the moving story of one woman's struggle to overcome poverty and oppression in order to live in dignity as an American Indian." She is part of a movement, spearheaded by the American Indian Movement, for native people to abandon the missionaries and go back to their roots—to fan the "spark of our ancient beliefs and pride . . . into a flame again," as she says in this selection. She says later in her book, "You should know that the movement for Indian rights was first of all a spiritual movement and that our ancient religion was at the heart of it." She is part of a radical rejection of the white men "who had brought us whiskey and the smallpox" and who had come "with the cross in one hand and the gun in the other." She says about herself, "I am a woman of the Red Nation, a Sioux woman. That is not easy."

THE RESPONSIVE READER

1. Mary Crow Dog's search for identity meant coming to terms with major conflicting strands in her heritage: being part Native American and being a woman. She had to deal with being half Sioux and half white and with growing up as a woman in a setting where men often thought women were good only for sleeping with them and minding the children. She is an "iyeska," half white and half Native American—who envied the "full-bloods" who did not need the sun to tan them. Reservation life forced her to be a survivor. Self-described as "ornery," she asserts, "I can hold my own in a fight."

2. Mary Crow Dog feels sorry for Native American men (although she feels "even sorrier for their women"). The men (or some of them) compensate for their loss of dignity and status by getting into barroom fights, going home drunk, and beating up their wives. In the past, the men "were famous warriors and hunters." They achieved a reputation by being generous and wise. They now have nothing to be generous with—they have no jobs and no money, and their traditional wisdom is ridiculed as superstition by "the white missionaries, teachers, and employers" running their lives.

3. The author says, "under the long snows of despair, the little spark of our ancient belief and pride kept glowing." The past was not totally forgotten because of the "courage and suffering" of those who tried to keep the flame alive. Oral tradition kept alive the stories of resistance, of the My Lai–like Massacre at Wounded Knee, and of the surrender or acquiescence of leaders like Chief Spotted Tail, who realized the futility of trying to stem the surge of the invading whites. However, the heritage and customs of the tribes, their "ceremonies, their sweat baths and sacred dances," survived among "untamed, unregenerated" people like the Crow Dogs of her husband's family, who refused to be "whitemanized." The land where the author lives is alive with the legends of her people (it is like the "winter counts," which were "picture writings on buffalo skin"). "You can't walk a mile" without coming across an old battleground or sacred hill: thus Crow Dog lives immersed among the relics and mementos of her people's story.

TALKING, LISTENING, WRITING

4. Many readers have found Mary Crow Dog an eloquent and impassioned voice for the current movement to restore the rights and dignity of Native Americans. She does not glorify the past or simplify the present—she speaks with equal respect of those who opted for surrender and those who opted for resistance? She eloquently appeals to her readers' sense of justice with her accounts of instances of genocide and of latter-day injustices like the forced sterilization of her mother.

5. Can today's generation be held responsible for the events and policies of over a hundred years ago? On the other hand, are we in some ways perpetuating the policies and attitudes of the past? One student wrote:

> "No man is an island," said John Donne in the seventeenth century, and that is as true at the threshold of the twenty-first. Just as "any man's death diminishes me," so too do injustices, both past and present, diminish us all.

6. Two contradictory impulses in the American tradition are the promise of free exercise of religion on the one hand and the desire to make America a Christian nation "under God" on the other. Are students ready to recognize Native American beliefs and rituals as a religion? Why or why not?

7. The author seems to have a shrewd sense of reality that keeps her from advocating a mere nostalgic dwelling in the past. For instance, women have to forge their own rightful place in what was a male-dominated native culture?

PROJECTS

8. Court battles over the desecration of Native American burial grounds or over "remains" in museums put our attitudes toward the cultural heritage of minorities to the test. Courts are reexamining ancient treaty rights. Ask students to search back issues of newspapers and periodicals for relevant material?

Maya Angelou, "Step Forward in the Car, Please"   39

Maya Angelou's *I Know Why the Caged Bird Sings* dramatized for a large audience historical patterns of racial discrimination but also the sources of strength that helped her overcome them. In this excerpt, we see her as a young job seeker coming to wartime San Francisco from the segregated South. She is determined to overcome the traditional barriers in a young black woman's path, and she becomes the first black conductor on the San Francisco streetcars. Her candid eyewitness account takes her readers beyond sociological generalizations and statistics to help them share imaginatively in the continuing struggle of America's minorities to claim their place in the sun.

THE RESPONSIVE READER

1. In this selection, we hear the candid voice of a determined, self-reliant person who steers clear of polemics and whose anger or indignation is well-controlled? She resolutely follows her mother's admonitions to carry on without self-pity or waste motion—even when other people might have lost their cool. ("My work shifts were split so haphazardly that it was easy to believe my superiors had chosen them maliciously"). Angelou speaks with a touch of irony that keeps her from being sentimental ("life was cheap and death entirely free") and with a touch of facetious hyperbole ("My room had all the cheeriness of a dungeon"). She has the detachment needed to look at her own emotions from the outside rather than being completely swept away by them: "From disappointment I gradually ascended the emotional ladder to haughty indignation, and finally to that state of stubbornness where the mind is locked like the jaws of an enraged bulldog." Angelou throughout sounds like someone who is very much "together" and who will not stoop to abuse or ranting but instead maintains a stance of cool superiority? (Note the way she talks about her immature classmates when she goes on to school.)

2. Racism here is not the work of crossburning fanatics or skinhead neo-Nazis. Instead, it is built into the everyday routines and habits of ordinary people, who hide behind innocuous-sounding excuses. The ploys range from the initial alibi of the receptionist ("they were only accepting applications from agencies") and the convenient and apparently continuing absence of the personnel manager to suspiciously weird work schedules designed to discourage the minority employee. In Angelou and her mother, the racism they encounter produces a dogged determination to carry on against odds.

3. Rock-bottom facts that emerge include the availability of conducting jobs, the trips to, and interaction in, the office, the eventual hiring, and the strange work schedules. Throughout there is a strong subjective element in the author's suspicion of the excuses and alibis (a suspicion she succeeds in making her readers share?). The writer's interpretation makes the minidrama in the office part of a larger familiar pattern—alternately seeing it as the impersonal operation of a racist system or blaming the individual involved.

TALKING, LISTENING, WRITING

4. Arbitrary barriers to employment and participation range from the exclusionary practices of fraternal organizations or of clubs without women or Jews to criteria making youthful looks a requirement for jobs as flight attendants or news anchors. We read about many current challenges to practices discriminating against women, Asian Americans, the physically disabled, and gays?

5. There is a strong element of pride in this account—and of "showing up" the people who stood in the author's way. But there is no vindictiveness or "getting even"? Angelou's major purpose was to encourage and inspire others?

6. Have students pool and compare relevant experiences in class.

7. Who uses which labels? Who brings changes about and why? Have your students ever been uncomfortable with the way they were labeled or classified?

8. Are your students ready to agree with what the author says about her mother's attitude during the daughter's search for work: "She comprehended that in the struggle lies the joy"?

PROJECTS

9. Challenges to discriminatory practices but also charges of reverse discrimination tend to swirl around eligibility for police work, for military service, for admission to medical school.

SUGGESTIONS FOR LANGUAGE WORK

Part of using the right word is to choose from among near-synonyms the one with the right shade of meaning. Why did the author use *dungeon* instead of just *prison, self-sufficiency* instead of *self-confidence, terse* instead of *brief, supercilious* instead of *superior, concoct* instead of *invent?* What does each word add that is missing from the synonym? (How is a charade different from acting something out? What makes an aphorism different from a proverb?)

Garrison Keillor, "Born Among the Born-Again"   45

Garrison Keillor is a teller of true stories in the tradition of the letter-writers and journal-keepers among his Unitarian Transcendalist forbears, who came to the vast spaces of Minnesota in the 1830s. His perennially popular radio programs recreate his childhood years in a Midwest of small towns, tightly knit families, and old-time religion. Mild eccentricity, gossip about neighbors, frank sentimentality, and folksy humor are staples of his cunning mix of nostalgic entertainment.

THE RESPONSIVE READER

1. Keillor opens his description of the Brethren with a vivid accounting of the tokens of their superior righteousness: "No clergyman in a black smock. No organ or piano. . . . No picture of Jesus." No hymnals or prepared prayers, and certainly no Popish distractions. An unprejudiced observer might be swayed by the "lovely silence" of the Brethren's Sunday morning gathering or the unadorned simplicity of the meeting or by the homespun wisdom of some of its members: "reading a prayer was sacrilege to us—'If a man can't remember what he wants to say to God, let him sit down and think a little harder,' Grandpa said." Brother Mel plays the role of the reformed sinner—who has seen the sinful world and then renounced it to testify to the superior virtue of the faithful.

2. Catholicism presents to the boy everything the lifestyle of the Brethren rejects and denies: spectacle, ritual, music, and symbols. "Everything we did was plain, but they were regal." The nineteen Brethren sit for service in the austere and quiet living room "while not far away the Catholics were whooping it up."

3. The story's high point occurs at Phil's House of Good Food, where the family's isolation from the ways of the world is highlighted. For them, the old devil alcohol turns the restaurant into a den of iniquity from which the virtuous beat a sad and funny retreat. They have no knowledge of restaurant etiquette: "For example, could a person who had been seated in a restaurant simply get up and walk out?" Outside, the boy exclaims that he feels humiliated, "like a leper or something." He then asks the question that goes to the heart of the matter: "Why can't we be like regular people?"

TALKING, LISTENING, WRITING

4. In a country with a strong tradition of religious fundamentalism, organizations like the ACLU watch jealously over the intrusion of private religious belief into the public sphere. The First Amendment to the U.S. Constitution prohibits the establishment of an officially sanctioned religion and protects the individual's right of worship. Emerging from centuries of religious wars and persecution, the young American nation opted for the separation of church and state. Should this tradition be interpreted to rule out prayer in public schools, nondenominational invocations at public ceremonies, the display of Christmas scenes on public property, and the like?

5. Freedom implies the right to be different. Is there too much pressure in our society for everyone to dress, think, and act alike?

6. Race, regional origin, ethnic roots, an unconventional family background, language differences, religious differences, and physical characteristics or disabilities are among the many factors that can create a sense of difference or isolation. (Note that for students to talk about such a subject freely requires trust in the ability of others to be sympathetic or respectful listeners.)

PROJECTS

7. Sample focus: What is or should be the role of parents? Is there a point where parents' insistence on instilling their own religious or moral values becomes indoctrination?

Susan J. Miller, "My Father's Other Life"   50

The context of this autobiographical piece is the extraordinary explosion of innovative "modern" jazz in the late 1940s and early 1950s.

To the author, the players were "Bird, Diz, Pres, Sweets, Al, Zoot"—
Charlie Parker, Dizzy Gillespie, Lester Young, Harry Edison, Al Cohn,
Zoot Sims. But the surface glamour of the jazz scene fades as we share in the
anguish of a family paying the price of the father's addiction.

THE RESPONSIVE READER

1. In her opening sentence, Miller takes us to the nighttime world of the
jazz clubs: "One night, at an hour that was normally my bedtime, I got all
dressed up, and my mother and father and I drove into New York." The jazz
club is in New York, and it is comprised of a "little stage" in a "smoky
nightlife room" filled to bursting with the cultural cognoscenti. The in-
crowd of musicians speaks a special language ("man," "cat," and "groove"
are examples of their "hip talk"), carries their saxophones and trumpets in
"battered horn cases," and shares in the addictions associated with the
nightlife world, especially heroin.

2. The opening sentence of the fourth paragraph is the turning point of
the essay: "As a child, I didn't know that my father and many of the musicians
who sat with their wives in our living room, eating nuts and raisins out of
cut-glass candy dishes, were junkies." It is at this point that Miller turns
away from her father's relationship with jazz and turns toward her father's
relationship with his family, profoundly affected by the father's addiction.

3. The impact of the father's addiction on the everyday lives of the
family is made poignant by the innocence and ignorance of the victims.
Miller did not know the truth until she was 21: "My parents succeeded in
hiding my father's addiction from us, but as a result, we could never make
sense of the strained atmosphere, our lack of money, our many moves." The
"addiction was the thread that tied everything together, but we didn't know
that such a thread existed, and so decisions seemed insanely arbitrary, my
mother's emotions frighteningly hysterical." The mother, in fact, was
"terribly depressed, sometimes desperate. I regularly found her sitting, eyes
unfocused, collapsed amid the disorder of a household she was too
overwhelmed to manage." As for the daughter, she lists two conflicting
responses to her father's drug experiences. On the one hand, she admires him
for rejecting the mores of the "white, middle- and working-class
communities where we lived" during the 1950s. "Part of me wanted to hear
them and love him—and indeed did love him for taking the acid, for taking
the chance." "But another part shut down, unable to care." Paradoxically,
Miller yearns for one of those boring fifties fathers who behaved in a more
predictable fashion.

4. The father's childhood so traumatized him that Miller cannot easily
condemn him for the choices he made in his adult life. "He would not have
been a good father even if he hadn't been an addict. By his own admission, he
came to parenthood ignorant of love and acquainted only with hate." His
mother, "the wicked witch of Brighton Beach," never gave her son any love or
encouragement, reserving all those qualities instead for her only other child,
the father's sister. The father's mother "despised men" and set out to make
her son's life one of misery and sadness. She fed "the fires of hate between

7

father and son, sister and brother," thus ensuring the father's misery was compounded by isolation. When the father was awarded some type of recognition, "She tore up a citation he'd won—and then spat on it." She kissed the father one time in his life and that was when he was leaving for war. The mother's last words to her son, cruelly forced upon him the night of his own father's death, were that she had left nothing to her son, "because he is no good."

5. The essay circles back to the father's love of music because in a life filled with disappointment, humiliation, and hurt, music, the father says, "is the only thing that's never let me down." Given the father's biographical background, it is perhaps no wonder that he turned to something non-human (music, drugs) to compensate for human failing and cruelty, but it is also true that the father's last words leave his family feeling, at the very least, diminished. "That the revelation would hurt us—my mother especially—never occurred to him. He never kept his thoughts to himself, even if it was cruel to express them."

TALKING, LISTENING, WRITING

6. How much should our knowledge of the father's own terrible childhood be allowed to mitigate our judgment of him?

7. Is such a situation a virtual rite of passage between parents and children?

8. The one-paragraph capsule portrait of Miller's father begins with the sentence, "My father was from Brighton Beach, Brooklyn, and earned his living dressing windows in women's clothing stores in and around New York City." The keynote of the portrait is the repeated theme of the father as a man who ate everything in sight, including himself. He was a man who "chewed his fingers, eating himself up" as well as a man who "constantly read, thought, and talked politics and culture, gobbling up ideas, stuffing himself as fast as he could—with everything."

9. Is there a range of perspectives on these topics? Or is there something like a dominant or prevailing media perspective?

Lois Phillips Hudson, "Children of the Harvest"   55

Lois Phillips Hudson describes an archetypal experience shared by many during the last century. She was uprooted from what seemed like a secure childhood world to join the hordes of migrants or refugees looking for a place to work, a place to live. Like the "Okies" of John Steinbeck's classic *The Grapes of Wrath,* she journeyed from the Midwest of dust storms and depression to the fields and orchards of the West, leaving behind life as a farmer's daughter to become a child following the harvests. Like millions of others in the modern world, she learned what it means to be unwanted, to be the alien looking for asylum in our midst.

THE RESPONSIVE READER

1. The young girl's reaction to the island in Puget Sound heightens the contrast between its green lushness and the dusty prairie she has left behind: "It always seemed impossible to me that we could be surrounded by so much water." The description of the hop field is especially striking. Hops are inedible, light as a feather, and sometimes "gummy with the honeydew of hop aphids." At times "tiny red spiders" would "flow up your arms, like more of the spots the heat makes you see."

2. Because the girl earns money by picking in the fields, she earnestly determines that the time has come for her "to assume a place of adult independence in the world." She is a wage earner, rather than just a girl doing chores on the farm, and she senses the connection between the ability to earn wages and escaping dependency. After she gives her sister three pennies, the girl feels "even more grown-up than before, because not everybody my age was in a position to give pennies to kids."

3. The experience of earning the first dollar, albeit for menial and undervalued labor, can be an eye-opener for the child trying to understand the ways of the world? After she has earned over a dollar for a day's picking, the girl feels she "truly comprehended the relationship between toil and media of exchange, and I saw how exacting and yet how satisfying were the terms of the world."

4. Probably to no one's surprise, there is here no real "equal educational opportunity" for the children of the poor. The author finds herself in a system in which "the pupils who were planning to attend this school all year were separated" from the children of the migrant workers. The workers' children, in their special classes, "did a great deal of drawing and saw a number of movies." Although the school at Wenatchee does not separate out the workers' children, it assumes that workers' children automatically belong in the lowest form. With the belated exception of the teacher at Wenatchee, no other teacher and no other school bothered to try to educate these children?

TALKING, LISTENING, WRITING

5. For instance, many families in our society have experienced being displaced by technological process making jobs obsolete, by factory closings in the "rust belt," or by gentrification driving them out of their neighborhoods? Many children of immigrants come from families that fled from repression or deprivation, leaving everything behind in search of a better future?

6. In most urban areas, many well-to-do children go to separate, aptly named "private" schools. Even in public schools, the children of the poor are likely to find themselves in a "vocational" rather than in an "academic" track.

7. Camps of migrant workers are often not officially recognized by the local authorities—and they often do not meet minimum standards. Illegal aliens are often part of an underground economy?

THINKING ABOUT CONNECTIONS

Both of these essays go counter to stereotypes about the work ethic as being the heritage of the white middle class.

SUGGESTIONS FOR LANGUAGE WORK

What words in this essay would send your students to the dictionary? How does the dictionary help them with words like *accoutrements, desultory, encroachments, mélange, elicit, unwonted, disconcert, inscrutable, incorrigible, augment*?

Frank Chin, "Donald Duk and the White Monsters"   64

Frank Chin is an aggressive, irreverent Chinese American author who writes about Chinatown youths in search of their own authentic identity— while navigating between obtuse elders, white prejudice, and gang violence. One reviewer said about Chin's novel *Donald Duk,* "Frank Chin's unique literary recipe—red hot chop suey laced with laughing powder and amphetamines—makes most so-called 'modern' writing look old-fashioned, chauvinistic, and tedious." Perhaps the keynote of this selection is sounded when the author says about Donald: "He doesn't like Chinatown. But he lives there."

THE RESPONSIVE READER

1. A stereotype, according to one student reader, "is a fixed mental picture of a person or group, held by a number of other people. Stereotypes are oversimplified opinions that do not allow for individuality and that reduce people to an assumed set of characteristics." (Have students in your class at some point or other rebelled against a stereotype?) Donald is critical of the stereotype presented of the Chinese by his Berkeley-trained California history teacher: "made passive and nonassertive by centuries of Confucian thought and Zen mysticism . . . the timid and introverted Chinese . . ." etc.

2. Donald, in the fashionable phrase, is ambivalent about his Chinese background, particularly when attention is focused upon it. His name and his looks are "driving him crazy," "He doesn't like Chinatown," and the school he attends "is a place where the Chinese are comfortable hating Chinese." Donald "avoids the other Chinese" at this school, tries to steer clear of the

gangs in Chinatown, and listens quizzically to the advice of his father, who wants him to walk like John Wayne.

3. While Donald's Chinese American name is unfortunately also the name of a cartoon character, many other adolescents object to their names at one time or another. (And many do change their names to something less ordinary or ridiculous when they have a chance?) So too do many adolescents dislike their looks, fear gangs, and dream about living in a totally different setting?

TALKING, LISTENING, WRITING

4. Reactions to Chin's use of humor will vary (an understatement). His account of the encounter with the "gang kids," with their black tanker jackets, de rigeur chewing gum, white tee shirts, and baggy black denim jeans will, it is to be hoped, amuse even the terminally earnest?

5. Here is the key question in the current controversies about a multicultural society. Encourage students from other than a monocultural background to think about and tell their personal story.

PROJECTS

6. You may want to send students to book reviews located through *Book Review Digest* or through indexes for leading national newspapers and periodicals.

THINKING ABOUT CONNECTIONS

Lee's humor tends to be more gentle and wistful? It has less of a hard-nosed street kid's quality?

Janice Mirikitani, "For My Father"   70

Janice Mirikitani's poem is a sad memorial to her father, who was irrevocably altered by the forced relocation and the harshness of camp life. Tule Lake was one of a series of camps spread out over the western United States in which over 100,000 Japanese Americans (three-quarters of whom were native born, and thus citizens) were detained during World War II.

THE RESPONSIVE READER

1. The father's experience no doubt played an important role in the metamorphosis of what may have been a young outgoing person into a taciturn, burnt-out, disillusioned adult. "He came over the ocean / carrying Mt. Fuji on / his back / Tule Lake on his chest." The Japanese tradition as

represented by Mt. Fuji is here part of the burden the father carries? The father may have been eager to unload the burden of Mt. Fuji and begin anew somewhere. But whatever dreams of a new beginning or better future brought him to this country ended in the bleak, volcanic terrain of the Tule Lake internment camp.

2. The daughter remembers the father as a stern, unyielding, silent man who turned a desert into a strawberry field. When the daughter was caught stealing strawberries, her father's "eyes held / nothing / as he whipped us / for stealing." Rather than judge her father, the daughter appears to have tried hard to understand him and how he came to be the way he was. She recognizes the elements that affected her father's personality: the trauma of the Tule Lake camp, the Herculean labors involved in trying to make the desert bloom, and the poverty that forced him to beat his children for stealing the family's crop. In the last lines of the poem, the daughter's tone is forgiving: "to shield desert-like wind / from patches / of strawberries / grown / from / tears."

3. Strawberries in the poem are a symbol for what is beautiful, delectable, and desirable (and expensive), and they thus contrast with the severe desert. A desert is arid, dry, and windswept; a strawberry is cool, moist, and refreshing. When the desert is used to represent the bleakness of the father's life, the strawberry is the untouchable crop he harvests, yet another thing not available to him. The desert may be the father's final destination and the strawberries may represent all the joy, hope, and beauty that have been stripped from him as he approaches his arid last stop.

4. "Hakujin" are inextricably linked to the allusion to Tule Lake, since it was white people who forced Japanese Americans into internment camps. The racism and xenophobia of the larger white society is again alluded to when the poet describes her "wordless" father selling strawberries to adults, "whose children / pointed at our eyes." Finally, white society is more affluent than the father and his family, since it can afford to buy strawberries for breakfast: "they ate fresh / strawberries / on corn flakes."

TALKING, LISTENING, WRITING

5. Students may want to interview elderly relatives who remember cycles of poverty or persecution.

6. You may want to assemble a panel of students representing differences in social class and have them explore these questions.

THINKING ABOUT CONNECTIONS

What does it mean to be the "other" in our society? Are there predictable recurrent patterns of resentment or hostility?

CHAPTER 2

THIS LAND: Landscape/Cityscape   81

What is a typically American setting? For the immigrant and for the European observer, kaleidoscopic, hectic, larger-than-life New York City was often the gateway to America. For many others, the Midwest has often been quintessentially American. In the words of Walt Whitman, "No one, I discover, begins to know the real geographic, democratic, indissoluble American Union in the present, or suspect it in the future, until he explores these Central States and dwells awhile on their prairies or amid their busy towns." More recently, many observers have looked to California and the rest of the American West in trying to read the shape of the future. And many see the most truly representative American landscape in the anonymous interchangeable housing tracts and plastic shopping malls of suburbia.

Ursula K. Le Guin, "Along the Platte"   83

Le Guin has been called an "authentic wise woman," with a mind "strong, supple, disciplined, playful, ranging over the whole field of its concerns, from modern literature to menopause, from utopian thought to rodeos, with an eloquence, wit, and precision that make for exhilarating reading." Comprised of "some notes from a day and a half on the Oregon Trail," Ursula Le Guin's "Along the Platte" is an open-eyed, open-minded account of a trip through the Midwestern United States. Le Guin lives in Oregon and has family in Georgia, so "every now and then" she travels from "corner to corner" of the United States. In the words of a student reader, "she knows how to find beauty in the everyday practical world."

THE RESPONSIVE READER

1. Striking sights and sounds begin and end with the rivers—the Missouri, Nemaha, and Platte—and include the gigantic Union Pacific switching center over which "high floodlights far down the line make gold rivers of a hundred intertwining tracks." Memorable snapshots capture the authentic quality of a time and place: "Down in the deep shade of trees in high thick grass stand three horses, heads together, tails swishing . . . Summertime." Radio Ogallala's reminder, "now is the time to be concerned about the European corn borer," will for many readers have a special midwestern flavor.

2. We show that we care or that something matters when we care enough to know its name? Le Guin uses the right names of trees: willow, aspen, cottonwood. The cattle are in "pure herds of Black Angus, Aberdeen, Santa Gertrudis, and some beautiful mixed herds, all shades of cream, dun, brown, roan." There are "Polled Shorthorns . . . Hampshire Swine . . . Charolais . . . Yorkshire and Spotted Swine." She mentions the names of the rivers—

13

Nemaha, Omaha, Nebraska (from Eastern Siouan)—which are obviously beautiful to her. Descriptions showing a lively imagination are everywhere: mosquitoes so large that wrecking balls could be used to squash them, or the stiff wheat that "sticks up like a horse's mane cropped short," or rivers at flood traveling "way over the speed limit for rivers." Trees are "up to their necks in water." The grain elevators are the cathedrals of the Midwest; with their "high and mighty cylinders of white," they loom over the fields the way Chartres cathedral looms over the fields long before the traveler sees the town. The Hereford Bull reminds Le Guin of an angry, curly-haired Irishman (is this an ethnic stereotype?).

3.   When charged two dollars to picnic, confronted with the smugness of a town called Lexington ("All-American City," "All-Nebraska Community"), or forced to listen to the "patriotism" of the rodeo announcer, Le Guin responds critically. These instances suggest that her standards exclude narrowness, intolerance, divisiveness? In the episode of the rodeo, her love of American popular culture is clear from her description of the spectacle ("All the seats are good," "the power of the big Brahma bulls," "the barrel-riding girls are terrific") and her conclusion: "People who want matadors mincing around can have them, there's enough moments of truth for me in a two-bit rodeo." Her criticism centers on the announcer's appropriating the occasion to expound his intolerant, hate-filled "patriotism."

4.   Trains are practical because they efficiently and cheaply move people and interminably long lines of railroad cars loaded with goods—with a mininum of congestion and pollution. At the same time, since the railroad first crossed the open spaces, the escape and adventure it promises have been romanticized, and movies, books, and songs have celebrated the lure of the trains. Le Guin is tapping into this history.

5.   Le Guin is an interested and curious observer, for whom the people and the places she sees are not mere obstacles or annoyances on the way to somewhere else. She is a participatory traveler who writes down descriptions of the scenery, who consults her travel guide and talks with the people she meets, and who takes part in the way of life she observes (by stopping to contemplate roadside sculpture and going to the rodeo).

TALKING, LISTENING, WRITING

6.   What's typically American? Students might observe that many of Le Guin's sights and sounds are more typical of farming and ranching country than of urban America. However, the nostalgia for the wide open spaces and for a small-town America is everywhere. Country music thrives in the big cities. Hunting and fishing are everywhere in the daydreams created by advertisers. (Politicians exploit the nostalgia for a small-town world?)

7.   The revival of nationalism around the world (ethnic conflict in the former Yugoslavia and the former Soviet Union, neo-Nazis in Germany, etc.) vividly reminds us of the capacity for hate and violence that is the

reverse side of the coin of patriotism and national pride. (Does love of country necessarily imply hatred of others?)

8. What are typical "tourist attractions" in this country? And where do people go who do not want to act like tourists? (For those who have not traveled, Thoreau's, "I have traveled much in Concord" is a reminder that travel need not be physical movement; it can also be mental?)

9. The secret of successful writing from firsthand observation is: "Move in for a closer look!" For models, have students look at Le Guin's description of the barrel-riders, for instance.

PROJECTS

10. Do sophisticates frown on rodeos, country music, and other paraphernalia of rural America? Does anybody anymore go to county fairs and Oktoberfests? Are parades, homecoming pageants, and picnics passé?

SUGGESTIONS FOR LANGUAGE WORK

What is the effect of the author's occasional use of informal language? Examples: "enjoying the damfool thing"; "a lousy way to earn ten bucks"; "audience yipping and yahooing all the way." (The folksy language seems appropriate to the author's subject matter, because she is traveling through small towns—the language is friendly and social. In the words of one student, "informal language is important to her essay because it gives the reader a flavor of the midwest, with its prairies, cattle, and rodeos?"

William Least Heat-Moon, "The Emma Chase Café"   88

The editors of the *Atlantic Monthly* said, "Heat-Moon is in a sense two people, and he writes about our continent, its leaves of grass, its geology, and its denizens with both the canny worldliness of his Irish and English background and the mystical time sense of his Osage ancestors." In his report on his journey through Kansas, he does write about geology—the original settlers' fear of drought; erosion as the "primary geologic force in Kansas today"; and people living close to a cycle of "flood, erosion, and deposition." In this excerpt, however, he talks about people who know the city but who share the nostalgia for a simpler small-town and country life. Linda Thurston leaves the city and city life to open a café, a "haven of rest" in Cottonwood Falls. William Least Heat-Moon chronicles the story of her endeavor, "The Emma Chase Café."

THE RESPONSIVE READER

1. Local history cannot provide Linda Thurston with a woman who is a feminist and an achiever to serve as name and ideal for the café. Local

history revolves mainly around the efforts of men. For example, the daughter mentions that her father started a newspaper and her brother wrote travel books—although this account also mentions a woman who was elected mayor. The woman running the café, Linda Thurston, is 39, a feminist "depressed" by the retrogressive social policies of the Reagan years, who has come back home in hopes "the Hills could heal." Her friend, Linda Woody, also in retreat from Reaganism, joins her, and the cafe "became unofficially the Retreat for Burned-Out Social Activists." The two women personally experience the same phenomenon that the women's movement as a whole experienced: "Women seemed in retreat from action to the easier, safer battle of awareness." After the frustrations and often apparent futility of fighting for beleaguered social causes in the city, it was therapeutic to work on a small scale with things susceptible to visible improvement: remodeling the café, preparing good food. A year later, however, both women are back in action in the larger social sphere—the one as a NOW lobbyist in Washington, the other as a university professor in rural special education.

2. Small-town life here has an authentic human touch missing in the anonymous, strife-ridden city? In the small town, the lack of privacy is compensated by a supportive community; change is discouraged by complete participation of the people in the community; and although radicalism is non-existent, some eccentricity is tolerated. Everyone knows everyone; people need one another for company and comfort; they cannot afford the exclusiveness and divisions of the big city. Because Linda Thurston is a native of the country, she understands the small-town ways and customs, accepts the things she likes, and works to change what she cannot accept. The women confront racism and sexism directly, but generally they "did not flaunt their politics." We do get glimpses of the ugly underside of country life: A "wealthy lady" claims there are "no battered women" in the county, yet some were afraid to inquire about services for battered women at a health fair. The women were afraid a neighbor might conclude they were abused.

3. Part of the women's dream was to provide a place with homemade bread and with coffee in real cups, but at the same time they introduced politically correct vittles like alfalfa sprouts? A restaurant can apparently be a laboratory for new attitudes and awareness, as when the new waitress is admonished not to present the check for a couple automatically to the male. Sexist and racist jokes are discouraged, and the refrigerator sports homey mottoes like "The rooster crows but the hen delivers the egg." The connection between food and politics is summarized half-seriously in their motto, "You can't start a revolution on an empty stomach." These women use food and the restaurant in part as a vehicle for their feminism, hoping to "undermine a few stereotypes along the way."

4. This need not be seen as a story of defeat? The price Linda Thurston paid—in money and in falling behind in her profession—was offset at least in part by what she gained. She was able to attempt her fantasy of "running a homey little restaurant," she "was at home for the last two years" of her father's life, and she was allowed the chance to live in the country as part of a closely knit community. Most importantly, perhaps, her feminist outlook

broadened: "Now I think feminism means being connected with other people, not just with other feminists."

TALKING, LISTENING, WRITING

5. Since the women here can be accepted by the locals as basically some of theirs who went to the city and came back, the attitude of the townspeople to real "outsiders" may not really have been put to the test. "Gossip and scorn" as the prime enforcers of the social mores might prove too stifling for many?

6. Do your students know someone well who seems like a fixture in a place? Some possibilities: oldtimers in a small town, a part-time salesclerk in a shopping mall, a short-order cook in a diner, someone running a boat for sightseeing or sport fishing, a janitor at a school, a family farming part-time.

7. Students might take their clue, for instance, from the local farmers' reaction to alfalfa sprouts: "They know silage when they see it."

PROJECTS

8. In a college town, especially, the decor and menu of a restaurant may make a statement?

Camilo José Vergara, "Our Fortified Ghettos"   96

Vergara takes off from a horrifying incident in Detroit, where seven children, ranging in age from nine years to seven months, were trapped by fire and killed in their house. Had the windows and doors not been fortified against the pervasive violence, the children might have been able to escape.

THE RESPONSIVE READER

1. Vergara dramatizes the issue of life in the ghettos by beginning with specific details ("At 2258 Mack Avenue on Detroit's East Side there stands a 120-year-old gray wooden cottage, a former farmhouse") about a terrible event that would not have happened elsewhere. It is hard to imagine a similar situation in a leafy and safe suburb, because, to begin with, house windows would not be barred in such a place. Vergara makes abstract and impersonal statistics meaningful when he translates them into terms of human misery. A statistic of ghetto children dying in house fires becomes wrenchingly meaningful when it is presented in this way: "LaWanda Williams, 9; Nikia Williams, 7; Dakwan Williams, 6; La Quinten Lyons, 4; Venus Lyons, 2; Anthony Lyons, 7 months; Mark Brayboy, 2." Striking details of the enormity of the tragedy are "a bright yellow tricycle parked in the weeds; a table with a large clock, its hands stuck at 2 o'clock, the time of the fire, and next to

it a neat line of children's shoes." There are pictures of "three angelic children" and "four ovals, each framing a cross" to represent the others.

2. After Vergara finishes with the story of 2258 Mack Avenue, he states his thesis as the opening of the fourth paragraph: "Fortification epitomizes the ghetto in America today, just as back alleys, crowded tenements and lack of play areas defined the slum of the late nineteenth century." The windows of 2258 Mack Avenue are gone, "but the metal bars are still visible." "Buildings grow claws and spikes, their entrances acquire metal plates, their roofs get fenced in, and any additional openings are sealed, cutting down on light and ventilation." Windows are rare and the air is stale: "In schools and in buses, plexiglass, frosty with scratches, blurs the view outside." Vergara closes this paragraph by linking fortification with inequality and institutionalized neglect. He says, "Throughout the nation's cities we are witnessing the physical hardening of a new order, streetscapes so menacing, so alien, that they would not be tolerated if they were found anywhere besides poor, minority communities. In brick and cinderblock and sharpened metal, inequality takes material form."

3. "In the ghetto," Vergara observes, "form does not follow function so much as it does fear." The extreme measures taken to protect buildings and property "announce the existence of a state of urban war." Government agencies, such as post offices, exist in "squatty concrete blocks with iron grating." A far cry from the "classical buildings decorated with eagles and images of the old Pony Express," the only "unifying national symbols" of these post offices "are the American flag on the outside and, on the inside, the F.B.I. most-wanted poster." Protective measures taken by businesses include "a fenced roof, blocked windows and a jail door," plus the omnipresent "razor-ribbon wire." One former shop owner was quoted: "even if his clothing store were housed in an all-steel building with no windows or doors, burglars would still find a way to enter and clean him out. 'They'd take cutting torches and do it and never get caught,' he reasoned." Churches are forced to "turn into fortresses." The ironically named "Lighthouse Gospel M.B. Church in Chicago gets a little daylight through a cross made of glass bricks." Of private individuals, "just about everybody keeps a gun." Non-apartment residents "surround the borders of their property with fences enclosing the house and family car. In addition, they bar their first floor windows and often install clearly visible burglar alarms, red lights blinking." Apartment dwellers live in heavily fenced ("topped with razor-ribbon wire") enclaves where "as many as four locks" are used in the "dangerous projects" and guard dogs are on the alert for "suspicious movements."

4. The people in this environment "feel powerless in their cages because they believe that crime is out of control." In a touching and heroic response to their world, they "strive to soften the unfriendliness of their environments, decorating homes and businesses with lively paintings, ornate wrought-iron designs and plantings." However, beneath this surface, "the fortress remains." "Isolation and a sense of imprisonment" result from blocked doors and windows through which no light can pass. The amount of time spent "opening and closing so many locks and gates, connecting and disconnecting alarms, nervously looking over one's shoulder" comes at the

expense of other activities. Extra money must be spent by people already financially threatened to fortify their homes and compensate for the lack of light and air that results from such fortification.

5. Paradoxically, the fortress mentality denies residents their best chance to improve their lives: The isolation that results means that the people are unable to try a social solution. "The most effective defense is not physical," Vergara notes. It is "social, as people watch after one another's dwellings, question strangers and call the police." This type of social response is a plausible strategy against crime-plagued and barred and boarded neighborhoods. Hopeful signs are the joyous life which continues inside the fortresses, from "the best meals of any shelter in the city" to the "great basketball games," to the "always busy" public library.

TALKING, LISTENING, WRITING

6. The degree to which the fortress mentality has shaped life in the most dangerous neighborhoods may come as a shock to students from more sheltered places. On the other hand, many students will realize that survival strategies have become part of city life generally.

7. Students might write about how they would fortify and protect the place where they live if conditions were to deteriorate.

PROJECTS

8. Task forces focused on gangs might be a starting point.

Jon Roush, "Square Space"   103

Roush weighs in on the side of nature lovers and environmentalists against the traditional American impulse to tame and civilize the wilderness. Nature, Jon Roush points out, is not something that can be divided by superimposing on it straight lines and right angles. Nonetheless, a glance at any street, city, state, or national map testifies to the strength of that impulse.

THE RESPONSIVE READER

1. The bison that wandered away from Montana's Bitteroot Valley was ostensibly a "domestic" bison. By putting the word *domestic* in quotation marks, Roush subtly introduces the point of the bison anecdote and of his essay. Bison are not domestic animals and never will be. Furthermore, nature will never be made domestic via the use of lines and grids. Despite the fact that the spaces in this country are no longer wide open, bison and nature are not going to conform to the human attempt at total control. This is illustrated by the errant bison's trail: "Yesterday he was seen in an irrigation

ditch, today he was in someone's vegetable garden, and so on. Fences were a minor annoyance. When he did not find holes, he made them." Roush is derisive toward the "overdressed" hunter, the "prime-time stalker," who shot the bison from thirty yards away by using a gun that was "scope-sighted." Even the hunter, Roush says, "might have sensed some absurdity" in his situation, but justifies his behavior with a particularly dense remark: "He told the cameras that since the hunt was legal, it must be sport."

2. Squareness becomes an issue in the article when another bison crosses the imaginary line that separates Montana from Yellowstone National Park. Once the bison enters Montana, he ceases to be a wild creature and becomes fair game for hunters who are participating in Montana's winter bison hunt. "One minute he was in wilderness, the next—bam!—civilization." Roush continues: "The absurdity that the bison did not understand, the absurdity that required his death, is the absurdity of laying straight lines on nature." When we lay straight lines on nature, we divide nature up into evenly sized squares. Such squares conform to "the mind of nineteenth-century America" by appearing to impose order upon the land. "Once it had been ruled into interchangeable squares, the vast western space could be controlled from Washington and New York." As a result land could be "bought and sold before the actual boundaries were even laid out. It was ready for the homestead acts. It was ready to expand, township by identical township, into an empire."

3. Unlike a city like Boston, whose "meandering maze of streets follow the ungeometric logic of real human community," the Western town did not have the luxury of time, nor did it have the experience of history. "Western towns were laid out for pure future, no past," in an attempt to establish "manmade order on the wilderness." Older cities are concentric; newer towns are linear. Typically, these towns were established along a single main street that "led from the prairie, through town, and back into the prairie." Looking at the road as it led out of town, "you could see the horizon. You saw the town's future prospects were infinite. A good town is still sprawling outward." People living in these towns were not trapped by James Joyce's "nightmare" of history; they looked only toward the future. Such people would have to believe in the artificially produced order that such towns imposed upon the land.

4. As the towns in the West imposed order upon the landscape, "people started talking about national parks. It was time, some said, to wall the wild in, to protect it from the incursions of civilization." Once the last bit of wild land was divided neatly, "the busy townspeople could be aware of wilderness, visit it, even revere it, without letting it interfere with business." Thus, the townspeople "put the bison in square parks and the Indians on square reservations." However, to experience nature from the air-conditioned comfort of a recreational vehicle while driving along perfectly straight roads is the antithesis of the wilderness. Roush points out we have "caged ourselves" in "compartmentalized spaces." We sense something is missing: "A fully civilized life includes more than law and order. It includes mystery, diversity, surprise, and beauty—the qualities that make natural space nourishing and occasionally dangerous." As we have removed such qualities

from our lives, we belatedly realize that the "rigid fragmentation of western space has walled us away from essential parts of our own being."

TALKING, LISTENING, WRITING

5. Roush does acknowledge that we have made progress in the way we respond to nature: "A hundred years ago, we would have known what to do about those stray bison. We would have rubbed out the whole herd in a weekend. Now we hesitate, uncertain." At bottom, Roush wants us to re-evaluate the way in which we implement wilderness and city planning policies. Straight lines and squares are not a realistic approach to a natural setting. In the Eastern United States, "surveyors had used a system of land description based on metes [boundary] and bounds, in which boundaries are often described in reference to actual landmarks."

6. Your students may suggest the car, the train, or the highway as alternative symbols for the way the "march of civilization" tamed the American wilderness.

7. In Europe, the Green or environmentalist parties, once mavericks on the fringes of the political scene, are becoming part of the mainstream. Their thinking is affecting the outlook of many ordinary citizens. Is something similar happening in this country?

THINKING ABOUT CONNECTIONS

Ursula Le Guin and William Least Heat-Moon celebrate at least some aspects of small-town American life. Le Guin's story could be described as a nostalgia trip through rural America; Least Heat-Moon's is the story of new thinking and new lifestyles becoming part of small-town life. Roush's essay is a more searching look at the underlying philosophy defining the conflict between our control-oriented civilization and the imperatives of trying to live in harmony with nature.

Harvey Milk, "A City of Neighborhoods"   107

After three unsuccessful campaigns, Harvey Milk was elected in 1977 as the first openly gay candidate for the San Francisco Board of Supervisors. His goal was to save his district, the Castro, from twin evils: He fought against redevelopment that turns organically grown neighborhoods into wastelands of office towers and against the poverty and decay blighting many American cities. In "A City of Neighborhoods," Milk contends that "the American Dream starts with the neighborhoods." If things are going to improve in our cities, it will be as a result of neighborhoods that preserve "the warmth, the touch, the meaning of life."

THE RESPONSIVE READER

1. In spite of decades of vaunted technological progress, our society has retrogressed as far as the well-being and happiness of its citizens are concerned. Poverty, unemployment, and the fear of violence are ravaging our cities. As Milk says, "Isn't it strange that as technology advances, the quality of life so frequently declines?" We have the most advanced sophisticated machinery, but people are sleeping in the streets under newspapers. We have sparkling clean homes with the latest appliance, but other people are afraid to visit our homes because the streets are a battle zone.

Business has to learn the elementary lesson that without employed customers fully functioning as human beings business cannot prosper—and goods will stay on the shelf. Milk says businesses "have a debt and a responsibility" to the customer and that businesses must realize that "the care and feeding of their customer" is only slightly less important than the needs of their shareholders. An integral part of "the cost of doing business" is helping the cities. Cities are essentially a part of a company's physical plant, and a company should therefore look after its city with the same investment, diligence, and commitment it uses to maintain its physical property.

2. Milk sees that the city he loves is changing—the traditional middle-class family has left for the suburbs; the population mix includes singles, young marrieds, retired people, the poor, the unemployed and the unemployable. For him, the ideal city is a place where people live instead of just come to work. It is run by people who live in it, who like city life, who prefer neighborhood stores to sterile plastic malls, who attend plays and eat in the city's restaurants. It is a place where people worry about education "even if they have no kids of their own." Once it has been recognized that the city has changed—"the demographics are different now"—the critical ingredients in Milk's vision of the future will be "new directions, new alliances, new solutions for ancient problems." For Milk, those who live in the suburbs and aspire to run the city (or serve in the police there) are "carpetbaggers."

3. The standard of living measures wealth and material things—technological advances that ostensibly make life easier, and technological products like television and "the latest appliances." But many of these "advances" create a sterile, sanitized lifestyle that impoverishes rather than enriches our "quality of life." We spend hours in front of a TV set—cut off from the smell, taste, touch, and feel of real life. In the "urban battlegrounds" in which we live, neighbors are afraid to mingle and talk, so we wind up "alone and unhappy in the vast wastelands of our living rooms." Sitting outside and talking with one's neighbors has no monetary value and does not figure in the Gross National Product but it is more valuable than slouching in a living room chair, watching "a make-believe world in not-quite living color."

4. Milk has a transparent sympathy for ordinary people (rather than the high and mighty), championing those who are impoverished by unemployment and those living in dangerous areas. He lectures businesses about not treating

customers as second-class citizens and not treating cities as "disposable," and he celebrates city life, "where the smell of garlic travels slightly faster than the speed of sound." Have we become too jaded and defeatist about the problems of the cities to respond to his generous vision of a city fit to live in?

TALKING, LISTENING, WRITING

5. Ask students who have some inside knowledge of the workings of government or business to talk about their experiences?

6. Perhaps Milk should be seen as both realist and idealist—with an idealism grounded in neighborhood realities. Don Quixote, the man from La Mancha, had read too many romances of chivalry and set out search of chivalric adventure—tilting at windmills while imagining himself in battle against formidable enemies. The naive idealism of Don Quixote clashes with the cruelty and meanness of the world. The quixotic vision transfigures ordinary drab reality: Where Don Quixote sees the enchanted golden helmet forged for the Saracen King Mambrino, the reader learns that it is in fact merely a brass basin worn as protection against the rain by a simple village barber.

7. Have your students had experiences with viable or revitalized neighborhoods? (Do they know places where people can sit outside sipping coffee, walk in a city park on a sunny day, spend time chatting with neighbors, or attend live cultural events?)

8. Ours does not seem a time for grandiose visions or idealistic schemes? Have students talk about the pros and cons of concrete projects: magnet schools, homeless shelters, rock concerts in city parks, decentralized administration of public schools, rape prevention or rape counseling networks.

PROJECTS

9. How do city officials estimate the well-being of the community? What kind of statistics do they quote? Where else could an investigator turn—chamber of commerce? neighborhood organizations? police departments? Do the media play down or play up the city's problems?

THINKING ABOUT CONNECTIONS

It can be argued that in Le Guin, Least Heat-Moon, and Roush there is a common thread of nostalgia for a simpler pre-urban and pre-industrial rural America. But Vergara and Milk make a strong plea asking us not to forget or write off our endangered cities.

Oates called the fiction of a favorite author—Flannery O'Connor—"enigmatic, troubling, and highly idiosyncratic," and the same adjectives could be applied to her own stories. In many of Oates' stories, the country of the young is truly a different country. In uncanny fashion, this story mirrors a feeling experienced by many adults: Their basic impulse is to make the next generation over in their own image, but they find the younger generation to be almost an alien race with inscrutable motives and willful disregard of the standards and niceties of their elders. Gretchen in this story lives in a world of shopping malls and suburban homes, through which she moves like a somnambulist—unconnected, alienated, narcissistic.

THE RESPONSIVE READER

1. Mud, lack of sidewalks, traffic, and newly built (and often newly vandalized) buildings are striking features in Gretchen's suburban landscape. These features, plus the bulldozers, traffic detours, and muddy fields full of rocks and glass, are all connected: They are all symbolic of a land that is undergoing the transformation from open space into anonymous, sprawling suburbia? Gretchen's suburban environment seems to have no tradition, no center, no sense of community. This is a place where walkers trudge through mud, dodging cars that roar past on the highway. It is an impersonal place where houses are made of simulated brick and set upon artificial hills, and where there is no human interaction between the people working in the stores and their customers.

2. Gretchen is bored, alienated, hostile—a girl who "plods" through life without being able to muster enough feeling or energy even to act sullenly. Gretchen's disconnectedness from her life manifests itself in unhurried and deliberate acts of destruction. She dresses in a fashion that is a total rejection of "junior fashions" (let alone of the injunctions of the "Beauty Myth"), walking around in genderless "old blue jeans" and a "dark green corduroy jacket" that is worn out in places. In a world bordered by mud, she wears white leather boots and "doesn't care" about getting them clean again. Gretchen's acts toward others consist of pushing them out of her way. She does this twice at the mall, and when she is forced to participate in sports at school, she "sometimes bumps into other girls, hurting them." In the stores and bathroom, Gretchen is either stealing or destroying things. In fact she uses the things she has stolen to destroy other things: stolen lipstick smeared on a mirror, and then the lipstick and stolen toothpaste stuffed into the toilet, which is then blocked up. She gets little thrill from stealing and is unruffled enough about the vandalism she commits so as to appear unafraid of being apprehended. Do your students see her as a symbol of youth alienated from and rebelling against a plastic commercial society?

3. At school, Gretchen "plods" along, "unhurried and not even sullen, just unhurried." In sports "she just stands around, her face empty, her arms crossed and her shoulders a little slumped." She is not interested in school or sports, and apparently has made no friends in the six months she has lived

at "Piney Woods." She is apparently an only child, disconnected from her family: Her father is away from home for the weekend, and her mother, who also goes to the mall, "doesn't notice" when Gretchen spies her on the escalator. When Gretchen enters the house, she is following her Invisible Adversary and acts as though she is unaware that the structure she has entered is her house. She tracks mud through the house, throws her jacket "somewhere," and sits in front of the television to watch a show she has already seen. Even though she has been in the house just six months, it seems unlikely Gretchen would ever think of it as home. Her father is essentially absent. She and her mother go to the same place, but not together. In suburban style, the mother drives to the mall ("Gretchen sees a car that might be her mother's but she isn't sure"). Gretchen is a thirteen-year-old girl with time on her hands: "She has hours for her game. Hours."

4. The Invisible Adversary is part of a "game" Gretchen has created to fill the void in her life—to create a sense of drama and to act out her smouldering hostilities? The game creates a sense of menace and pursuit, and in her empty, ineffectual life the imaginary adversary gives her someone to defy, to threaten, to control, and to make suffer?

TALKING, LISTENING, WRITING

5. Do students recognize the symptoms of adolescent alienation and rebellion in Gretchen? How is her alienation related to or different from in that shown in the rock culture or in rap? Do your students accept vandalism as a fixture of modern urban or suburban life?

6. You may want to ask: Is the author's purpose to make us understand Gretchen and others of her generation? Are we supposed to judge her as a pathetic human being? Or are we given a chance to sympathize with her secretly if we share some of her feelings of alienation? Are we supposed to blame a soulless, sterile society that causes young people to whither and die?

7. Discuss with your students the role of perception, of point of view?

PROJECTS

8. For instance, "Where Are You Going, Where Have You Been?" with fifteen-year-old Connie, is one of Oates' most widely-anthologized stories.

THINKING ABOUT CONNECTIONS

A striking generational contrast separates the Depression-era youngster determined to overcome obstacles and make her way in the world from the unconnected alienated suburban zombie devoid of initiative.

Lorna Dee Cervantes, "Freeway 280"   120

One of Cervantes' best-known and most widely reprinted poems is "Refugee Ship." The refugee ship is *el barco que nunca atraca*—the ship that will never dock, the ship that carries people between a nostalgically remembered past and an uncertain future. In "Freeway 280," the poet visits a place that she once longed to be away from; she discovers that many things from her childhood are flourishing, unseen from the freeway.

THE RESPONSIVE READER

1. The speaker presents the freeway as a massive, intrusive presence that has crushed the houses and flowers in its path. It is forbidding and uninviting: "I scramble over the wire fence / that would have kept me out." A "raised scar" implies that the freeway has developed over an open wound, i.e., the land that has been leveled for construction of the road. The "windsounds" are fake because they are not the wind sounds produced by nature, but are instead a by-product of rushing cars.

2. When the poet left, she was eager to leave: "Once, I wanted out, wanted the rigid lanes / to take me to a place without sun." Now the poet is in search of a part of herself she left behind, and that part of herself is connected with the way of life that has been disturbed by the freeway.

3. If the part of herself that was "mown under" by the freeway is anything like the other things that had been flattened—"new grasses / wild mustard . . . old gardens"—it will prove to be "a loose seed." Because the grasses and gardens have "come back stronger than they were," so too might that part of herself for which the poet searches.

TALKING, LISTENING, WRITING

4. The poet shifts to Spanish for names of things that were part of her childhood world and that she always used Spanish to describe: types of trees, little houses, vegetables, and herbs. She uses affectionate terms like viejitas—the old ones. At the end of the poem she again shifts into Spanish when talking about the search for her heritage: "Maybe it's here / en los campos extraños de esta ciudad / where I'll find it."

5. Much writing romanticizes and sentimentalizes a golden childhood world—while other writing dwells on the traumas and abuses of childhood?

PROJECTS

6. Bilingual Americans may use their native tongue at home with older relatives (but not with their children?). In strongly ethnic neighborhoods, business may also be transacted in the first language. Increasingly, radio and television programs cater to speakers of a language other than English?

26

CHAPTER 3

NEW WORLD: Diversity and Community   129

The revival of nationalism and tribalism around the world is reminding us that untold millions of Americans came to this country to leave behind the fratricidal ethnic, racial, and religious divisions of their past. Central to American history is the process by which large masses of immigrants—first mainly English, Irish, and German, then increasingly from Eastern and Southern Europe, and today predominantly from Latin America and Asia—moved toward full participating citizenship as Americans. This process of Americanization—the forces driving it, its drawbacks and limitations—has in recent years been the subject of much debate. What is the price people from diverse backgrounds pay for assimilation? Are there reasons why the "Melting Pot" theory of acculturation cannot work for large numbers of Native Americans, of Mexicans and Puerto Ricans, and of African Americans? Is it possible for people to be bicultural—to maintain strong ties to a distinct ethnic tradition while at the same time being fully American?

This chapter brings together essays that explore the rich mosaic of the American tradition. They call for greater recognition of diversity, or warn us not to lose sight of the common center, or project a future when a new ethnically mixed population will make old identities and oppositions obsolete. The chapter includes the personal testimony of first-generation and second-generation immigrants confronted with conflicting definitions of who and what they are.

Anna Quindlen, "The Mosaic vs. the Myth"   131

Anna Quindlen represents what disgruntled conservatives think of as the "cultural elite" of the liberal news media. She represents enlightened or right-thinking current social ideals, leaving behind the traditional definitions of Americanism that required immigrants and minorities to strive to make themselves over on the WASP model. As she visits PS 20 in New York City's Lower East Side, she observes the new "American mosaic" in the making, as pupils from the four corners learn to become Americans while each carrying with them differences that will ideally enrich their adopted country.

THE RESPONSIVE READER

1. In the melting pot, assimilation works toward a melting down of differences in language and cultural background, with the children of immigrants adopting a common culture of teenage slang, American popular music, baseball, McDonald's hamburgers, and diet cola. In its more aggressively chauvinistic version, the traditional melting-pot theory implied the gradual disappearance of "hyphenated Americans." A mosaic, on the

other hand, is made up of many different, yet equally integral, pieces that work together to form the picture or design. It is a more apt description because it recognizes the unique contribution of each cultural or ethnic strand to the overall picture of this country and because it validates the desire of people from diverse backgrounds to retain ties to their heritage. Quindlen says, there are "plenty of us who believe we lost something when we renounced ethnicity."

2. Xenophobia—the distrust of or antipathy toward foreigners that is easily mobilized by demagogues—is an old, resilient response to newcomers, particularly virulent when times are bad. In this country, xenophobia derives from the vision of an "authentic American," who is "white and Christian (but not Catholic), ethnic origins lost in the mists of an amorphous past, not visible in accent, appearance or allegiance." People who depart from this model are outgrouped as not one of us and encouraged to stay with their own kind. Xenophobia has found successive targets in the (Catholic) Irish, in Jews, in Italians (called "wops" and "dagos" by the bigots), in Asians ("the yellow peril"), and in Mexicans and Puerto Ricans from "south of the border."

3. Quindlen forges links between America's past and the present waves of immigration by quoting an 1835 treatise, "Imminent Dangers to the Free Institutions of the United States through Foreign Immigration." In 1835 xenophobic attacks targeted "such riffraff as Jesuits." Then and now immigrants were accused of not wanting to give up their own language or their own national identity. Quindlen upholds the traditional American ideal of America as a refuge for the tired, the poor, the "huddled masses," who come to this country where the Statue of Liberty lifts the "lamp beside the golden door." For Quindlen, "the true authentic American" is aware of the many ethnic strands in our common past (as she is aware of her Italian ancestry). The true American does not identify with a small exclusive Anglo-Protestant strand that traces its ancestry to the (capitalized) Pilgrims of Puritan New England but instead is represented by "a pilgrim with a small 'p,' armed with little more than the phrase 'I wish. . . .'"

TALKING, LISTENING, WRITING

4. Why are ties to different ethnic or cultural traditions stronger in some families than in others? Where have your students encountered pride in a separate cultural heritage, and what forms does that pride take? What organizations, programs, or institutions help promote it or keep it alive?

PROJECTS

5. Suggest the usefulness of interviews with elderly relatives or family friends.

SUGGESTIONS FOR LANGUAGE WORK

Quindlen's column is reprinted in mass-circulation newspapers around the country. What level of vocabulary does she expect in her readers? Would your students have to look up words like *amorphous, resilient, xenophobia, riffraff,* and *pejoratives?*

Oral History

José Luís and Rosa María Urbina, "Coming Back Across the River"   134

This is the story of Mexicans illegally crossing the river separating the American city of El Paso and the Mexican city of Juarez to work and live illegally in the United States. The comfortable cliché of a "nation of immigrants" here becomes harsh reality in the everyday struggle of this couple and their children. Al Santoli's interview with José Luís and Rosa María Urbina describes their attempt to survive and prosper in the United States.

THE RESPONSIVE READER

1. This is the familiar story of immigrants with little command of the language coming into the country (often illegally) to work at the most menial jobs—housework, construction work, work in the fields. Although in some ways their living conditions were better in Mexico (more space), Rosa says, "In the United States there is a lot of work, but in Mexico we have nothing." As for many others, the dream of a land of plenty remains elusive for these immigrants. In the words of José, "The dreams that Rosa María and I had of living in the U.S. and reality are not the same." What may be new and thought-provoking for many students are some of the givens of these people's everyday lives:

They live in constant fear of the immigration authorities (the migra), with raids rounding up illegal or undocumented aliens. The immigrants play a constant game of cat and mouse with the border patrol, with arrests, deportation, and almost instant illegal return part of "routine procedure." There is a whole underground economy of people arranging for the hiring and transportation of illegal workers. The working day often includes up to six or seven hours of bus rides to the workplace. New immigration laws are a constant worry—to be eligible for amnesty, people need records of employment and evidence of residence that illegals find hard to get. Questions: Why would the landlord be so generous, and how could the farmer have taken taxes and especially social security deductions from the wages of an illegal alien? At times, both José and Rosa sound rehearsed and too careful; this may be a result of the translation from Spanish to English or this may reflect their ingrained caution as illegals, subject to deportation at any moment.

Possibly interesting sidelights: There seems to be little personal animosity toward the border patrol or police (some are mean, others considerate). The landlord is generous and understanding.

2. The gender roles in the story seem quite traditional? José goes out to work in the fields, and Rosa does housekeeping jobs or looks after her newborn son. What is not traditional is that José had to leave school at twelve to help support his family while his sisters continued their education. His parents, José says, "chose my sisters to study."

TALKING, LISTENING, WRITING

3. José (contrary to bigoted stereotypes of immigrants milking the welfare system) will accept any work as long as it is work. As with other Americans, education for the children is a high priority. The Urbinas would like to become American citizens; all they want, José says, "is to be able to work in peace." However, José has "never learned to speak much English," and Rosa probably hasn't either.

4. The American tradition has been to take in and try to assimilate people looking for a new beginning. On the other hand, the people in this account have no legal claim, and resentment against a flood of immigrants is being stoked by politicians. At the same time, these people could not live and work here without the tacit, implicit complicity of the border patrol and of farmers and other employers relying on cheap, nonunion illegal labor?

PROJECTS

5. What do your students know about the byzantine immigration laws and procedures? Legal entry into the United States often becomes possible when a would-be immigrant has family members here, when an immigrant has a skill the country is in need of, or when an immigrant has sufficient capital to start a business that will employ other Americans. Those seeking asylum from persecution by their own governments are also eligible. Laws restricting immigration largely to people of European ancestry have long since been rescinded. Patience and time, as in the past, are required in vast quantities of any person wishing to immigrate legally.

Arturo Madrid, "Diversity and Its Discontents"   140

In "Diversity and Its Discontents," Arturo Madrid speaks for the "unmeltable" minorities whose looks and speech (and names) tend to make them seem "other" to mainstream Americans. Like many current writers, Madrid sets out to make a virtue of diversity, asking us to make sure that all of our institutions, and in particular higher education, reflect our respect for "cultural, religious, social, political, and even linguistic difference."

To help students follow and digest this very substantial essay, you may want to focus discussion in turn on three major dimensions of the essay: the history of the Southwest, with a native Spanish-speaking population and with Americans as newcomers; the author's personal sense of being different from mainstream Americans; the author's analysis of the lack of minority representation in higher education.

THE RESPONSIVE READER

1. Because Madrid does not "fit those mental sets that define America and Americans," he describes himself as the "other." His looks and speech make people ask him where he comes from—ironically so, since his people lived in the Southwest before the arrival of the Americans who gradually came to dominate the economy, the educational system, and the media in his region.

2. The *americanos* came into the predominantly Spanish-speaking Southwest as immigrants and missionaries, stripping the locals of their land. They came to dominate all aspects of society and the media—newspaper, newsmagazines, books, radio, and television. Artists, refugees from the cities, and atomic scientist became implants in the traditional culture. At the same time, the *americanos* refused Madrid entrance into their ranks with a "pervasive and systematic denial" that he was an American.

3. The unkept promise of the American educational system was that members of minorities would be accepted by the white majority if they mastered mainstream English. The myth of school was that it would erase Madrid's "otherness." Ironically, it was there Madrid felt his "otherness" the "most acutely." The central agenda of the school was socialization—acculturation. The students would learn to be Americans—by saluting the flag, reciting the pledge, and learning English. If students "learned to speak English well and particularly without an accent," they would "be welcomed into the American fellowship." However, Madrid learned that skin color and looks—pigmentation and physiognomy—remained key factors in outgrouping people of his background.

4. Like many others, Madrid at first downplayed his minority identity and status. He speaks of the "protective colorations" people use to disguise or camouflage their otherness: They ape the speech, dress, or mannerisms of the white majority; they change their names. As a young student, the author wanted to become what he saw as the American norm. However, he has spent the second half of his life "wrestling to understand" the "complex and deeply ingrained realities" of his cultural or ethnic identity and "striving to fathom why otherness denies us a voice or visibility or validity in American society." His aim now is not to deny difference but to "make otherness familiar, reasonable, even normal to my fellow Americans."

5. In New Mexico, where Madrid grew up, many professionals, business people, and officials were *hispanos.* However, when Madrid went to UCLA as a student and then to the East for his first teaching job (Dartmouth), he discovered that Hispanics, along with other minority groups, "were truly

missing persons in American institutional life." Thirty years, later, this "phenomenon is not as pervasive as it once was." Unfortunately, what has happened to the minorities who tried to participate in institutional life is "ghettoization, marginalization, isolation." Few are allowed in by regular channels (using the front door), and they do not get very far when they do. Others use various side entrances and find themselves cut off from influence and advancement. "Inclement weather" in the form of budget cuts and layoffs hits minority hires hardest.

6. The United States, Madrid says, "is the essence of diversity." In addition, "one of the principal strengths of our society" is a serious effort to solve the "economic, political and social problems" that have arisen. We will need that strength to make certain that "the extraordinary changes" occurring in our society result in equal opportunities at every level for everyone. We must make sure that "quality" or excellence is not narrowly defined as the special province of one limited ethnic or cultural tradition but that instead it is redefined to recognize and validate diversity. It is this diversity that "makes us a unique, dynamic and extraordinary nation."

TALKING, LISTENING, WRITING

7. Madrid speaks with bitterness about the unkept promise of traditional assimilationist schools and about the systematic exclusions of minorities and women from positions of influence in academic life. But he sees partial progress, and he sketches a vision of a more integrated society of the future?

8. How much contact do your students have with members of cultural or ethnic groups different from their own?

9. "What are you?" and "Where are you from?" are questions that make many people uncomfortable or resentful. On the other hand, at different stages in their lives, people may identify or rediscover a part of their heritage that they had tended to ignore or deny.

PROJECTS

10. On many campuses, charges of bias in hiring and retention have been given much publicity. Detailed affirmative action or equal opportunity guidelines have played a major role in job searches but are now under attack.

SUGGESTIONS FOR LANGUAGE WORK

Madrid's vocabulary ranges far beyond informal talk. However, he uses formal language or "book words" not in order to impress the reader but to sum up ideas essential to his argument. You may want to work with your students to show what key terms mean in the context of the essay. Examples:

"antedates Plymouth Rock" (Spanish-speaking settlers lived in America before the arrival of the pilgrims)

"*los americanos* were omnipresent" (the Americans, though new arrivals, were soon everywhere)

"more socialization than education" (the schools aimed at assimilating students to mainstream American society, at Americanizing them)

"ours was a proscribed language" (Spanish was banned; students were not allowed to speak it)

"however excellent our enunciation" (especially careful pronunciation)

"our pigmentation, our physiognomy" (skin color and facial features serve as indicators of ethnic or racial origin)

"his magisterial novel" (Ellison's *Invisible Man* is a masterly, authoritative treatment of the race issue)

"ghettoization, marginalization, isolation" (special programs for minority students or women may keep minorities on the margins or periphery of an institution, creating a kind of academic ghetto)

"America's demography" (changing distribution of ethnicities in America)

"the dark side of populism" (populist politicians speak for the interests but sometimes also the prejudices of the common people)

Diane Ravitch, "Multiculturalism and the Common Center" 149

In this essay Diane Ravitch makes the paradoxical assertion that the "United States has a common culture that is multicultural." She stresses the widespread recognition of the need for validating diverse cultural traditions while stressing the need for the common center. In her collection *The American Reader,* she participated in the search for the common center by reprinting entries that have "resonated in the national consciousness"—from Tom Paine's "The American Crisis" to Dudley Randall's "Ballad of Birmingham" and Lorna Dee Cervantes' "Refugee Ship."

THE RESPONSIVE READER

1. The general movement to recognize diversity has been away from the idea of assimilation in the melting pot and toward the idea "that variety is the spice of life." Embraced in schools and at university, the movement has led to a wide acceptance of the idea that we "must listen to a 'diversity of voices' in order to understand our culture, past and present." Ravitch seems

to assume that America has always had a "commingling" of diverse cultures, apparently seeing less of an exclusive dominant WASP tradition than her critics or adversaries. She talks about "America's relatively successful experience as a pluralistic society." Even with the qualifier "relatively," in light of the divisions and antagonism in our society, this may seem to many an optimistic assertion.

2. "Throughout human history," Ravitch observes, "the clash of different cultures, races, ethnic groups, and religions has often been the cause of bitter hatred, civil conflict, and international war." This is the basis for her warning that we must learn from the conflicts in our history how we have managed "to live together in relative peace and even achieve a sense of common nationhood."

3. Pluralism seeks "a richer common culture," that honors the rich diversity of the different cultural strands in our history. In a pluralistic society, "differences among groups are a national resource," and these differences enrich our common culture. Pluralism recognizes a rich multicultural tradition that is shared by all.

Particularism is the view "that no common culture is possible or desirable"; it teaches children "that their identity is determined by their 'cultural genes.'" Particularism is a kind of cultural separatism; it is a rejection of a mainstream American culture that is "'Eurocentric,' and therefore hostile to anyone whose ancestors are not European." Particularism is "ethnocentric" in that it encourages emphasis on a distinct ethnicity to the exclusion of other cultural influences.

Universalism, according to Ravitch, is the issue upon which "the conflict between pluralism and particularism turns." The universal appeal of great art and music—from Duke Ellington to Andres Segovia—transcends narrow ethnic boundaries. Particularism divides the United States into five cultures, one and only one of which should claim the allegiance of young Americans. The idea that the five could be combined into universalism is derided "as a form of Eurocentric arrogance." In response, Ravitch quotes the Roman playwright Terence: "I am a man. Nothing human is alien to me."

Among Ravitch's arguments against particularism: The classification of cultural backgrounds according to five major categories ignores the "huge cultural, historical, religious, and linguistic difference within these categories." (A category like Asian lumps together the many diverse ethnicities and religions of countries like India, Pakistan, China, Japan, Vietnam, and many others.) Intermarriage makes the typical American a person of mixed ancestry, who cannot be asked to opt for one ethnic tradition over another. Children need to learn mutual respect for different cultural traditions. Dividing Americans into descendants of "victims or oppressors" keeps "ancient hatreds" alive. The particularistic notion "that children can learn only from the experience of people from the same race" limits everyone's horizons.

4. Since Ravitch grants that "cultural democracy" has been recently evolving in our schools, she seems to recognize that a "Eurocentric" focus had for many years excluded the endeavors of others. Ravitch is not arguing in favor of the continuation of the "Eurocentric" monopoly; she is rather

pushing for more universalism in schools, at the expense of the particularistic position taken up by others. She does accept the supremacy of Western science.

5. The test case in this essay is that of a "Bolivian-born mathematics teacher in Los Angeles who inspired Hispanic students to learn calculus" by drawing on the Central American Mayans' contribution to mathematics. Students could thus gain self-esteem by relating to a non-Western tradition that is part of their own history. For many educators, this experiment seemed to show that Mexican American children will be attracted to science and mathematics if they study Mayan mathematics, the Mayan calendar, and Mayan astronomy. According to Ravitch, however, the teacher used the Mayan example as a pluralistic way to get the students' attention, but more importantly, he "required them to do homework and go to school on Saturdays and during the Christmas holidays." That, far more than the Mayan example, helped his students pass an Advanced Placement mathematics examination. However, this approach was adopted by some educators "as the key to simultaneously boosting the ethnic pride of Hispanic children and attacking Eurocentrism."

TALKING, LISTENING, WRITING

6. For instance, how dominant in the teaching of literature were Shakespeare, the English Romantic poets, etc.? What minority authors and Third World authors did your students encounter?

7. In cities like Chicago and Detroit, ties with old country traditions and lifestyles remain strong? With Polish-Americans and Italian-Americans, a strong nostalgic affection for ethnic tradition often seems to go hand in hand with an assertive patriotism as Americans?

PROJECTS

8. Disagreements over how far to move in the recognition of diversity often surface in the discussion of new courses, the revision of syllabi, or the consideration of textbooks with a strong multicultural dimension.

THINKING ABOUT CONNECTIONS

Use this and similar role-playing exercises to involve students in the give-and-take of current controversy.

Fox Butterfield, "Why They Excel"   156

This article is an example of the kind of journalism that eschews sensationalism, polemics, and excessive editorializing in order to present an informed opinion. On a subject clouded by clichés ("the model majority") and prejudice (an anti-Asian backlash), Butterfield draws on his personal experience, reading, and interviews to draw carefully supported conclusions.

THE RESPONSIVE READER

1. The idea of the model minority has received significant media attention in recent years. In many universities, programs in math, science, and engineering attract large numbers of successful, highly motivated Asian students. At the University of California in Berkeley, Asian students with top academic records gain admission in record numbers. (The chancellor of the university is also Asian.) The average per capita income of Asian Americans is higher than that of whites. Many run-down inner-city neighborhoods have been revitalized by the influx of Chinese, Vietnamese, or Korean businesses. By the same token, resentment against Asians among the urban poor has led to ugly incidents. Explanations or rationalizations for the relative success of Asian Americans range from genetics and parental expectations to a traditional work ethic and a traditional high regard for teachers and education.

2. In telling the story of Kim-Chi Trinh, Butterfield dramatizes the obstacles that would have defeated someone less determined or motivated, particularly during the nine-year-old's harrowing escape from Vietnam via the pirate-infested South China Sea. The obstacles she has overcome in her adopted country are formidable: a new language and a new way of life for a nine-year-old child, and "coping with a succession of three foster families." Filial respect and strong family ties emerge as key motivating factors; in the words of Kim-Chi Trinh: "I have to do well—it's not even a question. I owe it to my parents in Vietnam." Given what she has endured, her present place as a sophomore on scholarship at Cornell University confirms that her success is extraordinary.

3. Butterfield's statistics show that while Asian Americans "make up only 2.4 percent of the nation's population," they comprise approximately twenty percent of the undergraduate population at Harvard, MIT, and Berkeley. These numbers are indisputable evidence for the point Butterfield is making. His experts, reporting results from surveys that involved seven thousand children, confirm that "Asian-Americans consistently get better grades than any other group of students." This is attributed to several factors, including the motivation that Asian American parents instill in their children and the amount of time the children spend working on their schoolwork. Confucianism is cited as the source of the efforts by children to fulfill parents' expectations. The traditional philosophy encourages Asian Americans to work hard since a cornerstone of its message is that "man can be perfected through practice."

4. Three recommendations emerge from the article: (1) we must set a higher standard for our own children—"only 17 percent of Asian parents were willing to accept a C, against 40 percent of white parents"; (2) parents "need to become more committed to their children's education"; and (3) schools need to be reorganized to help students to enjoy school by arranging

recesses after each class and reducing the amount of time teachers spend lecturing. The first two recommendations are predictable, but the third one may be surprising. A teacher has the last word when he observes: "There are brilliant Americans in my chemistry class. But the Asian students work harder. I see a lot of wasted potential among the Americans."

TALKING, LISTENING, WRITING

5. and 6. Students will have varying answers to thorny questions raised by this article. For instance, is it true that as Asian students become more Americanized their achievement begins to slip? Can average American youngsters, raised on TV and pop music, be expected to emulate the work ethic of Asian American students?

7. In your students' thinking about academic success, what role is played by luck, biased teachers, unfair requirements, and the like?

8. The idea of equal opportunity becomes problematic when any one group, on the basis of merit, seems to secure a disproportionate share of college admissions, good grades, and access to graduate study. What other factors other than academic merit are we going to recognize in committing limited resources?

PROJECTS

9. As we try to understand the horrendous dropout/pushout rates in many of our schools, what factors are paramount—institutional, societal, familial, psychological?

SUGGESTIONS FOR LANGUAGE WORK

This article was published in the weekly magazine section of a big-city newspaper. What level of reading vocabulary did the journalist expect of her readers? Which of the following words would send your students to the dictionary: *diminutive, stereotype, ironic, discriminatory, disproportionate, intriguing, predictor, converge, instill, imbue, philosophy, sage, centripetal, rote learner?*

David Bernstein, "Mixed Like Me"   162

"Mixed Like Me" is David Bernstein's story of his first quarter century of life as "a twenty-six-year-old man, half black and half Jewish." At a time when many pundits see a sharpening of racial divisions and a flourishing of race politics, Bernstein projects a future when discrete racial and ethnic identities will be increasingly irrelevant. Bernstein's story and his proposed solutions to racial problems in America will confound many readers' expectations. Judging by the tone of this essay, Bernstein would enjoy knowing his readers had been discomfited.

THE RESPONSIVE READER

1. Bernstein's perspective on the strife-ridden racial legacy of the past combines a studied personal aloofness with much lively awareness of this country's racial history. He, personally, has not experienced racial discrimination: "I have not overcome racism or poverty, and people become visibly disappointed when I tell them that my mixed background has not been a cause of distress." However, glimpses of racism and race-related violence appear when Bernstein mentions the riots in Washington D.C. after Martin Luther King, Jr., was assassinated in 1968, and the two times in his life Bernstein himself was called a "nigger." He also mentions the destruction of a Jewish community center in Reading, Pennsylvania: it had "been bombed recently by Reading's prominent community of neo-Nazis." When Bernstein's parents married, miscegenation laws were still in effect in parts of the United States: "If they had lived then in the comfortable suburb where they now reside, they would have been breaking the law—miscegenation, as marriage between blacks and whites was known in those days, was still illegal in Maryland." Bernstein's mother "attended segregated public schools until senior high school, when she was in the first class that integrated Eastern Senior High School in the wake of the Supreme Court's Brown decision." His mother's brother "went off to fight in the Korean War, one of the first black airmen to participate in the integrated armed forces." (While this uncle was in Korea, "he fell in love with and married a Korean girl.")

2. Bernstein goes counter to stereotypes and expectations about race almost immediately when he tells us that his "mixed background has not been a cause of distress, or any other difficulty for that matter." Bernstein "founded and edits a conservative magazine that deals with race relations and culture"—also unexpected since neither Jews nor blacks have been strong in numbers amongst conservatives. His parents also confound expectations: "While their contemporaries marched for civil rights and held sit-ins, they hung out with a mixed-race group of cool cats at various jazz nightclubs in downtown D.C. Most of these establishments were burned to the ground after Martin Luther King's assassination in 1968, bringing to an end that unique era of naive integration." The entire essay can be seen as an exercise in stereotype-bashing, since it is the story of an apparently untraumatized, half black, half Jewish editor of a conservative magazine.

3. From his parents, Bernstein inherited "a healthy suspicion of conventional wisdom," and conventional wisdom in the case of Bernstein's "teachers and peers, was overwhelmingly on the left." His "political awakening" began in junior high school ("I was one of six kids in my junior-high class to vote for Ronald Reagan in our mock class election") and high school, where he "cowrote a piece in the school newspaper on what it meant to be conservative," which subsequently "nearly caused a riot." Once Bernstein realized "that you could make liberals mad just by saying the 'c' word," he set about with a vengeance to provoke such a response. For

conservatives, Bernstein was a godsend: "Other conservatives loved having me around. After all, most of them were presumed to be Nazis from the get-go by the ultrasensitive P.C. crowd; having a black person say you're okay was temporary protection from the scholastic inquisition." In addition, it was assumed that Bernstein had "special insight into why more blacks didn't identify with the Republican party," and Bernstein subsequently "began to believe that, somehow, I had special understanding of the souls of black folk, and with increasing confidence I would sound off about the political and social proclivities of African-Americans." To liberals, Bernstein "was living proof that imperialist, racist forces were at work, dividing black people and turning us against one another."

4. "There comes a time in every conservative activist's life," Bernstein says, "when he gets the heady rush of realization at how much fun (and how easy) it is to annoy liberals." Not surprisingly, Bernstein is a success at liberal-bashing; he had been training for the position since junior high school. People on the left are described as having "self-righteousness, humorless orthodoxies, and ultrasensitivity to their own and everyone else's 'oppression.'" Bernstein echoes familiar backlash sentiments against the "P.C. crowd," criticizing the "staleness of liberal beliefs, the inability of the campus activists to move beyond sloganeering to real thought, and the creation of a regime on campus by college professors and administrators that treats open discussion as anathema."

5. In the opening paragraphs of the essay, Bernstein declares, "For better or worse, America is going to look more and more like me in the next century—that is to say, individuals are going to be walking embodiments of the melting pot." The arguments over America as a tossed salad or cheese dip "will be made moot by the increasing incidence of mixed marriage and the growing class of mutts like me who have more ethnicities than the former Yugoslavia." Near the end of the essay, he returns to this theme: "In me, the melting pot the idea has become the melting pot the reality." Bernstein does not view the great diversity that is America as separate groups contributing something to the overall mosaic, or salad, or dip. He sees that great diversity made manifest in himself, and predicts that this is our future. In response to multiculturalism, Bernstein says: "The notion of 'self' should not be wrapped up in externalities like 'culture' or 'race'—unless you want to re-create the United States as Yugoslavia, Somalia, or any other such place where people's tribal identities make up their whole selves." "True self awareness stands opposed to grouping human beings along arbitrary lines like race, gender, religion, weight, or preferred manner of reaching orgasm." As regards groups, "the reality is that groups aren't equal; individuals are." "Groupthink" is described as "primitive," indicating lack of self-awareness and a "refuge for those afraid of differences."

TALKING, LISTENING, WRITING

6. Many familiar features of the latter-day young conservative—from cocksureness and extreme individualism to gloating liberal-bashing—are well illustrated here.

7. People of different persuasions inveigh against "divisiveness." How much of it do your students see in their own lives?

8. For instance, do members of the black middle class tend to be politically conservative? What about affluent American Jews or Cuban Americans? What about successful Asian Americans?

9. Have such labels come to seem increasingly irrelevant to students? Are there self-declared radicals on your campus?

PROJECTS

10. Do admissions offices, EOP programs, and other agencies keep and divulge such information?

Hisaye Yamamoto, "Seventeen Syllables"   170

"Seventeen Syllables" is the story of Tome Hayashi's three-month career as a haiku poet, and of the tension that arose because of it. Rosie, Tome's daughter, will never look upon her mother or father the same as a result of the short-lived success of "Ume Hanazono," the pen name of her mother. The rigid traditional Japanese mores regarding illegitimate birth and the refined upper-class traditions of Japanese poetry and formal manners are seen through the quizzical eye of a second-generation Japanese American narrator.

THE RESPONSIVE READER

1. Rosie is the archetypal second-generation American youngster, in transition between the old-country world of her parents and her new-world environment. She relates to English more easily than she does to Japanese: "English lay ready on the tongue but Japanese had to be searched for and examined." Although she has been going to Japanese school for years, Rosie has to pretend to understand her mother's haiku, for she is more interested in and comfortable with an English haiku with a factious touch. On the other hand, Rosie lives comfortably with her bicultural background. She reads her mother's magazines from Japan, enjoys visiting the four Hayano girls, and races up and down the tomato rows with her "great friend," Jesus Carrasco. At the opening of the story Rosie is a teenage girl who seems satisfied with the routines of her life. The biggest discrepancy between Rosie's world and her parents' more traditional world is that the person Rosie secretly meets is not Japanese American. In addition, at the Japanese school, Rosie amuses her friends with imitations of Fred Allen and Shirley Temple, and she sings "'Red Sails in the Sunset' at the top of her voice" while in the bath.

2. Rosie's father angrily brings his wife's poetic career to a halt after her poetic aspirations take her away from work in the fields. The central conflict in this story pits a simple man caught up in the world of work

against a woman who aspires to more. Rosie's mother blossoms as she responds to the refined language and manners of the poetry editor, representative of an upper-class culture beyond the reach of her peasant husband. The violent quarrel that results takes Rosie from the sheltered world of childhood to facing the antagonisms and violence of the adult world. Her parents' marriage was the means of Tome's escape from Japan and the humiliation associated with the stillborn birth of an illegitimate child. Mr. Hayashi, who had "lately arrived from Japan," agreed to a "hastily arranged" marriage that had been set up by Tome's sister in response to Tome's threat that she would kill herself if she stayed in Japan. As part of the bargain, the mother "kept house, cooked, washed, and . . . did her ample share of picking tomatoes out in the sweltering fields and boxing them in tidy strata in the cool packing shed." In contrast to a life filled with work, poetry offered Tome the opportunity to share in a lifestyle different from her own. All the father wants, in contrast, is to succeed with the harvest, visit a few friends, and play cards in the evening before retiring early.

3. At both the beginning and the end of the story, Rosie says what she is expected to say rather than what she feels. Each time she says, "Yes, yes," when she really wants to say, "No, no." As the story opens Rosie's real feelings are that she doesn't want "to disillusion her mother about the quantity and quality of Japanese" she knows. At times, she hates her parents, as when she wishes their Ford would crash and free her of her situation. At the story's conclusion, Rosie's feelings are that she cannot and will not promise her mother what the mother wants to hear.

TALKING, LISTENING, WRITING

4. The story reaches its violent climax in the quarrel between the mismatched parents whose loveless marriage was the result of an "arrangement." At the same time, the events are seen through the eyes of their daughter, for whom the strict mores and the refined art and poetry of Japan no longer have a vital meaning. The story can be read as a story of emancipation, as Rosie finds that she can identify with neither her father nor her mother but has to find her own identity?

5. Tome's story—the story of a woman trying to break out of the traditional role of the dutiful wife—has been a central theme of Western literature since Ibsen's *A Doll's House?*

6. Students are likely to have their own stories of parental expectations clashing with the need of the adolescent to become his or her own person. They may also have stories of incompatibility in mismatched marriages. They may have stories of the clash between the practical and the artistic temperaments.

PROJECTS

7. Some basic facts: Executive Order 9066 signed by President Roosevelt in February 1942 resulted in the arrest and detainment of

110,000 Japanese American men, women, and children, three-fourths of whom were native-born Americans. In 1944 the Supreme Court upheld 9066, and the internment ultimately lasted for more than three years. Japanese Americans, merely because of their Japanese ancestry, were wrenched from their homes and businesses and shipped to the desert to live in barbed wire enclosures.

Li-Young Lee, "Persimmons"   182

Having been born abroad, Li-Young Lee is closer than second-generation Americans to the world of his immigrant parents. The persimmons in this poem become a symbol of what he cherishes in his family and its traditions.

THE RESPONSIVE READER

1. The fruit appears in the poem first as a word that made the speaker stumble in the sixth grade, exposing him to ridicule as he mixed up *persimmons* and *precision*—with the poet, looking back on the incident, turning the tables on the teacher by linking the persimmon with traditions of precise knowledge and artistry. The unripe persimmon that the sixth-grade teacher brought to class is a symbol of the well-meaning, uninformed token gesture of the insular, monocultural mainstream American. The persimmon evolves into a symbol of life; the speaker's mother says, "every persimmon has a sun / inside, something golden, glowing." Finally, the persimmon comes back as the subject of one of his father's paintings, standing for the things that "never leave a person." The speaker finds two in the cellar, "wrapped in newspaper / forgotten and not yet ripe." The speaker puts them in the sun where they ripen and he gives the newly ripe fruit to his appreciative father.

2. Ironically, the teacher slaps the boy for getting the word *persimmon* wrong but then exhibits ignorance about the fruit by serving it, unripe and astringent, to the class.

3. The speaker has a bittersweet relationship with his father. The depth and sincerity of his love is tempered by the grim fact that the father will soon die. He is already blind and using a cane. The pictures rejuvenate the father and he becomes animated as he talks about them. The pictures evoke the past for the father just as the persimmons evoke the speaker's past.

4. Part of the bilingual learner's problem is that the ear does not recognize sounds or sound patterns not familiar from the student's first language. In addition, monolingual fellow students and teachers may tend to ascribe the bilingual speaker's limited proficiency to lack of intelligence—rather than crediting the immense achievement of a achieving even limited proficiency in a second language.

TALKING, LISTENING, WRITING

5. Students will appreciate the universality of much of the poem: the boy growing up, the father growing old, first experiments with sex, an uncomprehending teacher, etc.

6. For instance, a lost childhood home, a secret hiding place of childhood years, a first trip beyond familiar surroundings, or the discovery of a way of life very different from our own can become charged with memories and symbolic significance.

PROJECTS

7. Make sure students hear the poem read aloud; encourage them to project the nostalgia, loyalty, and affection that suffuse much of the poem.

CHAPTER 4

History books in school and college are undergoing sweeping revision as we reexamine and reevaluate the role and effects of European expansion and takeover of the New World. This chapter asks students in turn to listen to voices speaking for the indigenous people of the Americas, reexamining the charges brought by later generations (and some contemporaries) against the Spanish conquerors, paying tribute to pioneers who came not as conquerors but as people in search of a place to live, and honoring slaves who rebelled against their masters.

Suzan Shown Harjo, "I Won't Be Celebrating Columbus Day"   195

Harjo explains why she does not consider the twelfth of October an appropriate day for celebration. She sums up the case of Native Americans against "500 years of colonization." She calls for a reeducation of the "colonizing nations" and for effective measures to help Native Americans overcome poverty, disease, and low self-esteem.

THE RESPONSIVE READER

1. For Harjo, Columbus is not a symbol of a spirit of discovery but of the European invasion. For the native peoples, the arrival of the Europeans brought "bloodshed and destruction," amounting to genocide—the systematic extermination of whole peoples. The explorers were not searching for new horizons but for "India and gold." The white man's exploitation and ravaging of the land amounts to "ecocide." Native people were stripped of their land in centuries of "land grabs and one-cent treaty sales," in violation of solemn treaties. Harjo's tone is often sarcastic and provocative, as when she calls Columbus' voyage "the original rub-a-dub-dub lurch across the sea," speaks of a "five-century feeding frenzy," with the benefits to the native peoples amounting to "horses, cut-glass beads, pickup trucks and microwave ovens."

2. Harjo's contends that "the participation of some Native people" in the Columbus Day celebrations "will be its own best evidence of the effectiveness of 500 years of colonization." The argument over Columbus Day is not a matter of ancient history—the "deplorable conditions" under which many Native Americans live are the legacy of the history of conquest, as are the diseases from which they suffer in disproportionate numbers.

3. Charges of treaties broken and of holy sites or burial grounds violated have been widely publicized—and litigated. The objection to "stereotypes of us as sports mascots or names on leisure vans" is also familiar, with notable holdouts like the Washington Redskins and Cleveland Indians.

TALKING, LISTENING, WRITING

4. General education courses and textbooks are everywhere being reexamined and revised, with much controversy surrounding traditional Western Civ courses and the like.

5. You might want to arrange for a student panel with representatives of the pro and con.

PROJECTS

6. The research paper in Chapter 12 ("A Flawed Saint") takes stock of current controversies regarding Father Junipero Serra.

Gregory Cerio, "Were the Spaniards *That* Cruel?"   198

A key word in the first sentence of this essay is *ambivalent*. Many "Hispanics" or "Latinos" are of mixed Spanish and Native American ancestry. They are thus likely to respond with mixed feelings to charges of genocide brought against the Spanish conquerors. Gregory Cerio tries to clear his Spanish ancestors of charges that he traces to the fratricidal religious wars of the Reformation and Counter-Reformation.

THE RESPONSIVE READER

1. The conflict between Catholic Spain and Protestant European countries is a pivotal part of this essay. Only twenty-five years after Columbus' first landing, Martin Luther began the Protestant Reformation, and Charles V, King of Spain and Holy Roman Emperor, responded with the Catholic Counter-Reformation. The Protestant European countries, all of which hated the "prosperous, powerful and smug" sixteenth-century Spanish, created and fueled "la leyenda negra," the Black Legend, which was a "body of anti-Spanish prejudices." According to Cerio, we received our "cultural legacy from the same people—English, German, Dutch, French—who fought Spain for 300 years."

2. Strong points in the case Cerio builds are the evidence of genuine soul-searching about the fate of the Indians among the clergy (de las Casas) and evidence of concern with the legal rights of Indians at the Spanish court. But many of Cerio's attempts to make his readers see the behavior of the Spaniards from a sixteenth-century perspective may seem like rationalizations to the sceptical modern reader? Spaniards accepted traditional rationalizations of social hierarchy, believing with Aristotle that "large masses of humanity are simply born to serve." By the standards of the day, Spain "acted with moderation." The double motives for Spain's behavior in the New World were succinctly put forth by a soldier in the army of Cortes: "We came here to serve God and also to get rich." The subjugation of the native peoples was justified "in an age of devotion" by the

Spaniards' belief that they "offered the Indians a gift worth any earthly pain: eternal life in heaven."

3. Cerio defends the Spaniards against charges of genocide, claiming (as many modern historians do) that the native populations were decimated by the white man's diseases, against which they had no immunity. "When the English and French arrived in the Americas, they systematically drove the natives from their land," Cerio says. In North America, in many cases, the non-Spanish colonists "simply exterminated the Indians." The Spaniards intermarried, creating the mixed European and Native American *mestizo* race of Latin America.

TALKING, LISTENING, WRITING

4. Cerio provides a thought-provoking perspective in this article, since he challenges a familiar tendency to judge the past retroactively by the standards of the present?

5. Columbus and his contemporaries acted according to their own limited lights, with greed and religious fanaticism providing a potent mixture that may be hard for moderns to understand.

6. From Cinco de Mayo celebrations and salsa to the Latin American literary renaissance, "la raza" has in many ways penetrated the consciousness of Americans.

PROJECTS

7. Note that Cerio quotes Fuentes. Richard Rodriguez has in recent articles and a new book explored the ambivalent relationship between the North American and Latin American cultures. Octavio Paz has at times written in highly positive terms about the meaning of the U.S. experiment for other nations.

THINKING ABOUT CONNECTIONS

You may want to ask students to script and present an imaginary dialogue between the two.

Oral History

Black Elk, "The Earth Is All That Lasts"   204

Much of what we know about the original lifestyle and mindset of Native Americans has been filtered through the accounts of white historians, missionaries, or anthropologists. John Neihardt's *Black Elk Speaks* was the result of Neihardt's attempt to induce one of the last of the survivors to talk freely and at length about a vanished way of life and about the last battles of his people against the invading whites. Black Elk was a teenage boy in 1876 at the time of the events described in this selection. As transcribed by Neihardt, his account does not romanticize Native Americans in the latter-day Hollywood style but is filled with fierce loyalty to his people.

THE RESPONSIVE READER

1. The lifestyle of Black Elk's people is that of a community on the move, with elaborate customs surrounding warfare and worship. Ceremonies and customs include the "sun dance . . . to give the people strength" and "counting coup" by being the first to touch an enemy in battle. Black Elk's people practice self-mortification while tied to the sacred tree. Medicine men use "sacred herbs" in curing ceremonies after purifying themselves in sweat tepees. Women did much of the work: "The women chopped and stripped cottonwood trees during the day and gave the bark to the horses at night." These are the wives, mothers, and daughters of warriors, and they celebrate the bravery of the men. Black Elk shows his mother his first scalp and she "gave a big tremolo" for the boy when she saw it.

2. War in this society is traditionally an honorable and celebrated endeavor. "When the men paint their faces black, the women all rejoice . . . because it means their men are going to kill enemies." Of the tribespeople who were ready to give up the fight and who returned to "Soldier's Town" rather than join with Crazy Horse, Black Elk says: "We did not like them very much." Warriors shout "It's a good day to die!" and "Take courage, boy! The earth is all that lasts!"

3. Crazy Horse appears here as the idealized "great chief" fighting the invasion of the gold-seekers in the Black Hills. Black Elk speaks of his people's reverence for him: "They would do anything he wanted or go anywhere he said." A leader who leads by example, Crazy Horse is preoccupied ("he always seemed to be thinking hard about something"), aloof ("he never joined a dance"), and unacquisitive ("He never wanted to have many things for himself"). He was a leader who took no special privileges: "They say that when game was scarce and the people were hungry, he would not eat at all."

TALKING, LISTENING, WRITING

4. Students will have their own reasons for identifying or not identifying with Black Elk, and gender will probably be a factor. Black Elk's feelings about reaching for adulthood may seem universal, and the struggle of a doomed people against overwhelming odds may activate a strong sympathy for the underdog.

5. Dehumanizing or diabolizing the enemy was strongly in evidence in the war against the Japanese in the Pacific and in the war against the Vietcong.

PROJECTS

6. The Canadian *Black Robe*, chronicling the early contacts between the tribes of the Northeast and fanatical Jesuit missionaries, may come as close to an authentic unretouched but admiring re-creation of the lifestyle and mentality of not yet "whitemanized" native peoples as is possible for us today to achieve.

Irving Stone, "Death Valley Earns Its Name"   218

Stone brings to life the westward movement of the wave of white settlers as a major formative influence in the history of this nation. Whereas history books used to focus on the doings of generals, presidents, charismatic preachers, and "captains of industry," this account pays tribute to the anonymous many who ventured into the unknown and endured incredible hardships in the search for a place to live. Pioneer women, tougher than the men, emerge in this account as the unsung heroes of the westward movement.

THE RESPONSIVE READER

1. Apparently, as with the disastrous Donner Party's decision, the "more experienced mountain men" who led both expeditions allowed themselves to be overruled by more voluble and persuasive members of each part. Mrs. Brier, on the other hand, would never allow herself to be overruled or dissuaded: "Every step we take will be towards California" was her determined refrain. A hardworking, determined, religious "wisp of a woman," Juliet Brier's "inner strength saved not only her own family," but several other travelers as well.

2. The terrific courage and self-sacrifice of Juliet Brier are counterbalanced by the two single men in her party who "decided they would strike out alone in the hopes of saving themselves," and who took virtually all of the remaining food with them, since theirs was "the only flour in the party."

TALKING, LISTENING, WRITING

3. The pioneering mystique is still invoked in political oratory and variously credited with the spirit of self-reliance, independence, and enterprise that is part of traditional American lore. On the other hand, today's citified Americans will seem almost completely isolated from the desperate realities of this account: the uncharted endless treks toward

dubious destinations, the life-or-death search for water, the need to cope with the bleak and dangerous terrain, the struggle to stretch dwindling provisions, the determination to carry on as many perish in the heat of the deserts.

4. Have students share representative entries with the class.

5. Some possible motives for our abiding interest in documentary nonfiction: the yearning for vicarious experience taking people out of their relatively safe but boring humdrum lives; the fascination with the "what-if"? (What if we had been part of the group: how would we have measured up?) Documentaries and pseudo-documentaries ("docudramas") are a major part of the modern television viewer's and the modern reader's fare.

PROJECTS

6. Local museums and chambers of commerce should have information on pioneers and founders. Schools often involve students in local or regional history.

Matthew Kauffman, "The Day the Slaves Got Their Way"   224

The struggle between the pro-slavery forces and the abolitionist movement played a major role in shaping the self-image and conscience of the new American station. (The conflict that it helped engender almost destroyed the union.) Kauffman in this article reminds us of an uprising that for a time may have dwindled into a footnote in the history of the slave trade but has recently again become a symbolic of the universal struggle against oppression In 1839 slaves commandeered the schooner transporting them to the Americas. They then began an amazing journey across the seas and through the justice system of the United States.

THE RESPONSIVE READER

1. Some basic facts: The Amistad rebellion occurred in 1839 when fifty-two slaves aboard the schooner Amistad "rose up against their Cuban captors." In commandeering the ship, they killed four of the white crew but spared two others, ordering them "to sail east toward Africa." Unknown to the Africans, the Cubans turned the ship around at night and "spent nearly two months zig-zagging north along the East Coast, hoping to be rescued." The ship was seized in the summer of 1839. Pro-slavery forces expected the black men to be tried as mutineers and murderers, but the abolitionists made the case into a cause célèbre by claiming that the Africans were free men who had been illegally deprived of their liberty and had acted in self-defense against their kidnappers. The Africans were neither slaves nor criminals, the Supreme Court ruled in March, 1841. The Africans—after some instruction in Christianity and farming—returned to Africa ten months later.

2.   Needed background: Kauffman assumes that his readers know what the abolitionist movement was trying to achieve overall, that they have some understanding of U.S. courts and procedures for appeals, and that they can place these events in historical perspective, as the Amistad was seized over two decades before the beginning of the Civil War and twenty-five years before Lincoln's Emancipation Proclamation. When naming those associated with the slavery and anti-slavery forces, Kauffman expects some minimal recognition of names: President Martin Van Buren, "bowing to pressure from the Spanish Government," and "former President John Quincy Adams, who argued the case before the U.S. Supreme Court."

TALKING, LISTENING, WRITING

3.   Students are likely to recall a variety of sources, ranging from Booker T. Washington's *Up From Slavery* and Harriet Beecher Stowe's *Uncle Tom's Cabin* to the *Autobiography of Frederick Douglass* and Alex Haley's book and television miniseries *Roots*.

4.   Will most students tend to take the side of the slaves? Will any be ready to play devil's advocate?

5.   Note that decisions by school officials and school boards on similar questions have in recent years often precipitated energetic controversy.

PROJECTS

6.   Note that according to Kauffman only two of the nine members of the Supreme Court opposed slavery and that the president worked against the Africans.

Daniel J. Boorstin, "Why I Am Optimistic about America"   227

A widely published and far-ranging historian and popularizer of history, Boorstin here gives an affirmative, optimistic interpretation of American history. He thus goes counter to the soul-searching and revisionism of recent decades. For Boorstin, America has consistently been "the Land of the Unexpected." It is in this country's unique response to questions that had divided people for centuries that Boorstin finds reason for hope.

THE RESPONSIVE READER

1.   A booster is an enthusiastic, energetic supporter of a cause. Boorstin was raised in Tulsa, Oklahoma, a city that "thrived on 'booster' pride." Boorstin says, "I suppose I have never been cured of my distinctively American Oklahoma optimism, bred in the bone and confirmed by the real history of Tulsa." Admitted to the Union a mere ten years before Boorstin's

family's arrival, Oklahoma was a state full of optimism and bursting with energy. Tulsa was a dynamic city that at the time of Boorstin's graduation from high school "boasted two daily newspapers, three skyscrapers, houses designed by Frank Lloyd Wright and a public-school system superintended by the former U.S. Commissioner of Education." In high school, Boorstin "memorized and declaimed patriotic orations"—from Patrick Henry's "Give Me Liberty or Give Me Death" to Lincoln's Gettysburg Address. Boorstin's father "was one of the most enthusiastic 'boosters,' and the growing city seemed to justify his extravagant optimism."

2. The essence of "American Exceptionalism" (Boorstin calls it a "long word for a simple idea") is the belief "that the United States is a very special place, unique in crucial ways." "American Exceptionalism" is a cosmopolitan view of history because it draws on the experience of people from all over the world: "The modern world, while profiting from the European inheritance, need not be imprisoned in Old World molds." "American Exceptionalism" is an optimistic and humanistic view of history because it is hopeful that the people participating will be free of old prejudices and restraints and thus able to make a new start: "The future of the United States and of its people need not be governed by the same expectations or plagued by the same problems that had afflicted people elsewhere."

3. Boorstin catalogues the history of religious strife in the Old World: The Roman Emperor Nero used the Christians as scapegoats for the burning of Rome in A.D. 64. After the Emperor Constantine founded the Christian era of the Roman Empire in 330, Christianity maintained its hegemony for the next 1,200 years with inquisitions, persecution of heretics, and profligate corruption that led to the rise of Martin Luther. The bloodletting began in earnest once the Reformation was followed by the Counter-Reformation and nations began to align themselves with the new Protestant groups (e.g., John Calvin in Geneva, John Knox in Scotland) against Roman Catholicism. As the second millennium approaches, Catholics and Protestants in Northern Ireland may or may not be ready to cease fighting. The Spanish Inquisition was established in 1478 to persecute Jews and Muslims who were deemed to be insincere in their (often forced) conversion to Christianity. Among its leaders was the infamous Tomas de Torquemada. The St. Bartholomew's Day Massacre occurred on August 24, 1572, with the knowledge of the de facto leader of France, Catherine de Medici, widow of Henry II. It was an attempt to stamp out the French Protestants (30,000 killed) and reverse the growing influence of Calvinism. The Thirty Years War (1618–1648) was a seemingly endless struggle that pitted the Protestant German princes and France, Sweden, Denmark, and England against the Catholic German princes and the Hapsburg Empire. (The war killed close to half the population of Germany.) Boorstin notes that America has never actually waged war over religion: "Who could have predicted that the United States, unlike the nations from which our people came, would never suffer a religious war?" Americans of all religious backgrounds have lived and continue to live peacefully together. Furthermore, although "the U.S. would remain conspicuously a nation of

churchgoers," the nation as a whole would support the separation of church and state as a "cornerstone of civic life."

4. In Europe, languages came before nations. In Italy, Dante wrote his *Divine Comedy* in Italian in the early years of the fourteenth century; Italy did not achieve nationhood until the last years of the nineteenth century. The United States, on the other hand, was made up of people "willing and able to borrow a language," English, and fashion that language toward their own purposes. American English and the concept of America (an ongoing process) came together at almost the same time. The English language has been "invigorated and Americanized" by borrowing from many sources—from German: *kindergarten, zeitgeist, blitz, gestalt, ersatz, verboten;* from Italian: *graffiti, piazza, opera, gala, chiaroscuro;* from French: *envelope, cul de sac, rendezvous, reservoir, boulevard, deja vu, camouflage, facade;* from Spanish: *patio, plaza, mesa, burro, hacienda, guerilla, rodeo, matador;* from Yiddish: *schmuck, shtetl, pogrom, zaftig, kosher, kvetch;* from American Indian tongues: *tepee, pow-wow, moccasin, canoe, wigwam, totem, kayak, papoose.* Boorstin says that we should call Broken English "our distinctive American language, for it bears the mark of our immigrant history."

5. A constitution, Boorstin says, is "the tradition of a fundamental law," and the United States inherited from England the tradition of English Common Law, which dates "back to at least the 13th century." "The byproduct of a nation's whole history, the unwritten English constitution was a pillar of government and of the people's rights"; this tradition arrived at an American shore with the Mayflower. Approximately 175 years later, the essence of English constitutional law "would find a transatlantic written reincarnation in the deliberations of 55 colonials meeting in Independence Hall in Philadelphia in 1787." Boorstin concludes, "So our United States was created by a constitution." Regarding foreigners from other nations, Boorstin quotes Benjamin Franklin: "Strangers are welcome because there is room enough for them all, and therefore the old inhabitants are not jealous of them." In addition, the United States has never been conquered by a foreign power and subsequently occupied, as, say, the Russians were by the Mongols, then Napoleon's armies, and then Germany in the Second World War. As a result, "welcoming the newcomer as worker, customer, community-builder, fellow-citizen-in-the-making" has been "the mainstream of our history." Unprecedented features of the American tradition include a Civil War fought "in a struggle to free a subject people," and "strenuous effort," including equal opportunity laws and affirmative action programs, "to compensate for past injustices."

6. People come to America "not for wealth but for a better 'way of life.'" Wealth is an Old World concept, presumed to be finite and static, while the standard of living is a New World notion that blurs "the boundary between the material and the spiritual." The standard of living is described as a "characteristically American idea," and it is something not secretly hoarded; rather, it is "publicly enjoyed." Wealth is private possessions, while the standard of living is something that people share. Since the standard of living is a measure of "goods, housing, services, health, comfort and education," it is a concept that emphasizes community rather than

individuality. Such a concept would be unimaginable in the Old World, "burdened" as it is "with the legacy of feudal 'rights,' landed aristocracies, royal courts, sacrosanct guild monopolies and ancestral cemeteries."

7. To show how America's power in the world is different from the power exercised by earlier superpowers, Boorstin quotes the French writer Malraux and his reactions to the 1962 Kennedy White House. Malraux observed: "The United States is today the country that assumes the destiny of man. . . . For the first time, a country has become the world's leader without achieving this through conquest, and it is strange to think that for thousands of years one single country has found power while seeking only justice." Boorstin notes that Malraux might have added that the United States, in addition to seeking justice, was also "seeking community." He concludes that we must "see the unique power of the United States, then, not as the power of power, but as the power of example. Another name for history."

TALKING, LISTENING, WRITING

8. Boorstin pays only slight attention to prejudice, bigotry, or meanspiritedness in the nation's past. ("Of course there were dark shadows—like the relentless racial segregation, the brutal race riots of the 1920s and the Ku Klux Klan.") He stresses the blessings of religious peace, constitutional government, and multiethnic harmony that Americans take for granted but that millions yearn for in strife-torn and lawless parts of the world.

9. The "latent perils" that might jeopardize America in the future are "ethnic, racial and religious hate," which is once again flourishing in Europe and other parts of the world in an age of tribalism and holy wars.

10. Is the welcoming spirit dead in the cities but still alive in the country? Or are Americans generally hostile to people coming into the state, the city, the neighborhood?

PROJECTS

11. Newspaper coverage of religious minorities, cults, or the religious right could provide a starting point.

Ralph Ellison, "Mister Toussan"   234

Historical note: Haiti is the western part of the Caribbean island of Hispaniola. (Santo Domingo is the other part.) In the eighteenth century, Haiti was a French colony where African slaves labored on the sugar plantations. In 1791, mulattoes (Haitians from mixed marriages) rose against the Creole planters, who were native-born descendants of the original French settlers. Toussaint, a self-educated freed slave joined the uprising in order to liberate the African slaves. As the leader of the Haitian forces, he for a time fought successfully both the British and the French (the two colonial powers who were fighting over the island during the Napoleonic wars). He was finally captured by the French and died in a dungeon in France shortly afterward.

THE RESPONSIVE READER

1. Ellison fights the racial stereotypes presented in a school textbook ("The geography book says they 'bout the most lazy folks in the whole world"). The two boys, used to seeing black people in menial positions, discover a black leader who abolished slavery and as a successful general for years bested large colonial armies.

2. The boys delight in exuberant hyperbolical talk. Some of their exchanges move by way of an echo effect, with the second speaker picking up phrases from the first and then moving on. First Buster and then Riley act as the leader. The one who is not leading acts as a chorus, repeating words from the leader's chant or emphasizing the leader's emotion. For example: (Buster) "Down to the water, man. . ." (Riley) ". . . To the river water. . ." (Buster) ". . . Where some great big ole boats was waiting for 'em. . ." (Riley). They delight in role playing: "Come on, watch me do it now, Buster. Now I bet ole Toussan looked down at them white folks standing just about like this and said in a soft easy voice: 'Ain't I done begged you white folks to quit messin' with me?'"

3. The mother plays a traditional role: She sews for the white folks and sings in the choir. She has such a beautiful singing voice that "even old Rogan" from across the street "stopped rocking to listen." After the boys get obstreperous on the porch, the mother comes out and scolds them for confirming the stereotypes held by whites: "White folks says we tear up a neighborhood when we move in it and you-all out there jus' provin' them out true." She is too used to the existing structure to sympathize with the rebellious spirit brewing in the younger generation?

TALKING, LISTENING, WRITING

4. As the leader of the first large-scale organized attempt to abolish slavery in the Western hemisphere, Toussaint represents a turning point in the history of colonialism?

5. Some very successful television series (*The Cosby Show,* for instance) have been resolutely upbeat, presenting upscale African Americans in warmly humorous and endearing fashion. On the other hand, black exploitation films present a very different image of American blacks?

6. What experience have students had with initiatives like Black History Month? What is the story of the controversy about the Martin Luther King, Jr., holiday?

7. Students may have seen Spike Lee's movie about Malcolm X. You may want to suggest other names.

Poem

Louise Erdrich, "Indian Boarding School: The Runaways"   242

Louise Erdrich spent much of her childhood on a reservation in North Dakota where her father taught school. She has been very active dealing with issues relating to Native Americans, from land claims to fetal alcohol syndrome among children.

THE RESPONSIVE READER

1. The runaways are running away from the boarding school that has forcibly separated from their homes; they are fugitives from the dreary and unimaginative routine of punitive school life. In the past the runaways have unsuccessfully attempted to escape enough times so that they know the routine of capture. The system they try to escape stamps out color and individuality with regulation clothes and punishes the runaways with beatings, laborious work, and special clothes designed to shame the wearer.

2. The "lacerations" of the railroad tracks across the land mirror the "worn-down welts / of ancient punishments." The children in the freezing boxcar watching the open landscape "through cracks in boards" are like prisoners longing for freedom?

3. Phrases like "long insults," "ancient punishments," "delicate old injuries" echo through the poem like a refrain?

TALKING, LISTENING, WRITING

4. Forced acculturation—taking children from their families to make them over in the image of an alien society—is not a practice most students are likely to expect in their own country?

5. What explains the wide range of likely responses to this question? Is it a matter mainly of the students' individual temperament, of the students' willingness to conform to the expectations of society, of the difference between progressive and reactionary schools, of the difference between idealistic or sensitive teachers and martinets?

6. A key question—allow for open discussion and a range of views.

PROJECTS

7. Note that in relatively homogeneous suburban or private schools this may be less of an issue than in city schools.

THINKING ABOUT CONNECTIONS

Defiant pride and a strong sense of grievance provide common threads in these accounts. The arrival of the Europeans, the losing struggle against the invaders, and attempts to "civilize" and Christianize Native Americans are seen here from a very different perspective.

CHAPTER 5

OUTSIDERS: Unheard Voices   251

For a country traditionally committed to equal opportunity for all, a new Gulag archipelago of the excluded, the evicted, and the abandoned has become a challenge to conventional assumptions about the promise of America. Usually, the armies of the homeless, the convicts, and the mentally ill remain anonymous, without a voice. (The prison system, in the case of a writer like Dannie Martin, has at times gone to great lengths to silence the voice of a convict speaking for the men and women in our overcrowded jails.) The homeless and the ill often do not have the most elementary means of making their story heard. This chapter gives readers a chance to listen to such often unheard voices.

Anonymous, "Homeless Woman Living in a Car"   252

Diane, who once earned forty thousand dollars a year as an editor, now is homeless and seemingly trapped in an inexorable decline. She describes her predicament in this article. Since she is not lazy, irresponsible, or spaced out from drugs or alcohol, her story challenges the excuses of those who watch the spread of homelessness with complacency.

THE RESPONSIVE READER

1. Diane's fall into "the abyss" was caused neither by chance nor self-destructive behaviors. It was directly related to her living up to her responsibilities as an only child, the death of her mother, and "an aged father advancing steadily into the dementia of Alzheimer's." The correct combination of circumstances pushed Diane off her tightrope, just as the correct sequence of events could push anyone off.

2. Diane's homelessness is a consequence of her performing her filial duty. Her story defies the stereotype of the homeless, as she is not a drug addict, alcoholic, or mentally disabled person. This article thus expands one's thinking about the causes of homelessness.

3. Eschewing angry defiant rhetoric, Diane makes the problems, deprivations, and dangers of homelessness frighteningly real to the reader. Problems include finding a safe place to put her car for the night and trying to look for a new job without a telephone or permanent address. A staggering list of deprivations would begin with sleep, food, and washroom facilities, and conclude with "hot water, coffee, tea, drinking water, a newspaper, a restroom, my own chair and a place to leave the car." Diane's situation is dangerous because to stay in a place, she must "remain

invisible." The areas that afford invisibility are also isolated, and there "is danger in isolation."

TALKING, LISTENING, WRITING

4. Students with facile answers might be reminded that the cause of homelessness is ultimately the inability to raise a down payment and monthly rent. Housing affordable to people at the bottom of the social scale has shrunk as the numbers of the homeless have swollen.

5. Students living out of their cars do not usually advertise the fact. Former friends and acquaintances tend to shun those who have fallen between the cracks?

PROJECTS

6. Has society blotted out the homeless as the sight of people sleeping in doorways and foraging in garbage pails has become frequent and expected? Some communities have instituted aggressive policies designed to drive their homeless to other jurisdictions.

Lars Eighner, "My Daily Dives in the Dumpster"   257

While the anonymous author of the preceding article is still carrying on her losing struggle to rejoin the ranks of the housed, Lars Eighner, like many others, seems to have made his peace with having become a permanent member of the underclass of the homeless and unemployed. His concern is survival—as a scavenger using his wits and common sense as he conducts "My Daily Dives in the Dumpster."

THE RESPONSIVE READER

1. There are various scavenging tips offered here with the expertise and insider's detail one might expect in a TV program on French cooking: peanut butter is not perishable even when unrefrigerated; untrained help in pizza parlors results in the discarding of perfectly good pizzas with the wrong topping; watching the academic calendar leads one to a bonanza of uneaten food thrown out by departing college students. To be wary of "ethnic food" or other unfamiliar foodstuffs is obviously good advice for any who, like the author, guard against dysentery.

2. Although "there are precious few courtesies among scavengers," surprising tidbits of etiquette apparently exist: "It is a common practice to set aside surplus items" in a visible place. Scavengers will also respect individual garbage cans because this helps increase public tolerance. The writer has another, surprising, reason for not going through individual garbage cans: "This seems to me a very personal kind of invasion." In

58

addition, he feels it would be "unethical" for him "to draw conclusions about the people who dump in the Dumpsters." Can scroungers, on the other hand, in their single-minded concentration on cans they can sell for a few pennies, are the discriminating scavenger's nemesis: They "tend to tear up the Dumpsters, littering the area and mixing the contents."

3. Not surprisingly this article demonstrates that our society routinely and thoughtlessly discards much edible food and usable items (the way it discards people).

TALKING, LISTENING, WRITING

4. Eighner's insights are often delivered with mock seriousness and a zany satirical touch? He distances himself from the "rat race millions" because he is not interested in material things for which he has no use: "I find that my desire to grab for the gaudy bauble has been largely sated." He distances himself from his former government job by observing that, in contrast to government, dumpster diving "rewards initiative and effort." He concludes the article with a warning about "the rat race millions who have confounded their selves with the objects they grasp and who nightly scavenge the cable channels looking for they know not what."

PROJECTS

5. Innovative and heavily promoted recycling campaigns are evidence of our slowly increasing awareness of our wastefulness. Nationwide, programs to reduce landfill volume have been implemented. Publications, lunchbags, and paper towels are made partly from recycled newspapers. And so forth.

Dannie M. Martin, "An Overcrowded Maze"   261

Dannie Martin became somewhat of a folk hero to First Amendment supporters when he defied prison authorities who were trying to silence him. He received a thirty-three-year sentence for an attempted bank robbery in a society where murderers and perpetrators of multimillion stock frauds may be released from prison after a few years.

THE RESPONSIVE READER

1. Most thought-provoking and real in Martin's accounts of his fellow convicts are the "subterranean activities" that arise as a result of overcrowding and the combative attitude of newly arrived convicts, who have lengthy mandatory sentences and therefore nothing to lose. By opening his account with the stabbing, Martin simultaneously grabs the reader's interest and dramatizes the level of savagery in his "maze." The story of the twenty-year-old bank robber illustrates how much anguish the errors of the

authorities can cause the convicts (like putting the wrong man in isolation), how the overcrowding at prisons is actually life-threatening, and how "tough new sentencing laws," designed to make politicians look good, will press "bewildered newcomers and cage-wise cons" into a lengthy co-existence that will ultimately benefit no one. One common thread in stories about the "get tough" sentencing laws is that they make prisoners more antisocial and heedless; they also exacerbate the overcrowding, which will in turn cause more convict "introversion, secretiveness, clique mentality, violence and deceit," hardly "the traits society wants to foster" in men who will ultimately rejoin it.

2. By reporting convict dialogue and the details of daily prison life, Martin takes the reader into the hidden world of prisons. "Inside-story" aspects of the article are the particulars of life within a small cell, "the climate of lawlessness," and the secret codes and signals prisoners use. A waiting list for the isolation building (another result of overcrowding) and the lines for food, phone, laundry, and visits are additional effective details.

3. Martin is comparing convicts in overcrowded prisons with mice in an overcrowded cage. In a laboratory study of the results of overcrowding, mice exhibited "cannibalism, self-mutilation, aggressive behavior (to the point of attacking any moving object), sexual ambiguity, introversion and homosexual behavior." Martin presents these results in tandem with quite similar daily behavior in his prison.

4. Martin's article ends with a warning. Most convicts will return to society eventually, and some of those who have served long sentences in overcrowded prisons "are going to make Freddy Krueger look like an Eagle Scout." If for no reason other than its own safety, society must conclude that change is necessary?

TALKING, LISTENING, WRITING

5. Prison and camp authorities have often hidden the inmates behind a wall of silence. Students' views may range over a spectrum on the issue of whether imprisoned human beings have a right to have their feelings considered and their views heard.

6. Although the pressures of overcrowding often force authorities to release prisoners early, the idea of rehabilitation has been abandoned by many?

7. Martin's articles made many readers imagine themselves perhaps for the first time in the convict's shoes. Did reading this article have a similar effect on your students?

PROJECTS

8. The last few decades have been bad times for idealistic advocates of prison reform. How familiar are your students with the fashionable "lock-them-up-and-throw-the-key-away" rhetoric?

The mentally ill, abandoned by fair-weather friends and shunned by society like the lepers of the Middle Ages, are fortunate if they retain as a last anchor the loyal support of their families (who are often told to "let go"). Frank, in "Memories of Frank," is Mary Kay Blakely's adored elder brother. This article describes Frank's "nervous breakdowns" and how they affected his sister and the rest of his family.

THE RESPONSIVE READER

1. Diagnosed as "manic depressive" by the doctors, Frank "thought of his illness as a spiritual fever." Blakely reports he had his first breakdown or episode the year he left home. He endured seven more in "his brief adult life," and committed suicide in 1981. Frank's family suffered from the fear of mental illness ("Every one of my siblings lived with his fear") and from dread that they were somehow responsible for Frank's condition. The family coped by actively participating in Frank's treatment and trying to fathom the cause of his illness.

2. The article explains that the shift toward a biochemical explanation for mental illness, especially manic depression, had begun to occur by 1970. Experiments had revealed "faulty genetic wiring," which suggested that "biology, not socialization, triggered the disease." A muscle enzyme had been identified "that seemed to play a role in manic depression." Biochemistry started to replace Freudian psychiatry as the key to treating mental illness.

3. Blakely's anger shows through most clearly when she describes the futile weekly psychotherapy sessions. "I hated the Thursday night sessions, when the patients and their families were collectively grilled under the harsh fluorescent lights of the locked ward." The toll this exacted on her parents is immeasurable: her father, "in despair . . . doubting himself, believing a dozen more hugs might have saved his son from madness."

4. Society is concerned mostly with shielding itself from people with mental illness. We get glimpses of a newspaper columnist who has no sympathy for Frank and a neighbor of Blakely's who is frightened by him.

TALKING, LISTENING, WRITING

5. Ironically, lithium carbonate, which failed to stabilize Frank's moods, has worked successfully for many patients. New medications like Tegretol have enabled many others to return to normal, useful, functioning lives, doing for them what insulin did for diabetics.

PROJECTS

6. Families struggling against the catastrophic consequences of mental illness encounter various forms of Catch-22. The ACLU, for instance, has successfully worked to disallow hospitals and doctors the option of detaining or treating patients without their signed consent. (This would be an enlightened precaution if the patient could be assumed to be in control of his or her mental processes, in which case he or she is not likely to be in the psychiatric ward in the first place.)

Jo Goodwin Parker, "What Is Poverty?"   275

Poverty, which once may have seemed to be becoming obsolete in an affluent society, has made an appalling comeback in recent years, especially among single mothers and their children. "The poor are always silent," says Parker. Her classic essay has for many readers broken that silence.

THE RESPONSIVE READER

1. Soap, hot water, sheets, "proper underwear," proper garbage disposal (no shovel!), medication, and all but the most monotonous and cheapest food become unattainable luxuries for people whose welfare payments cover just barely shelter and not so much food as malnutrition.

2. For this single mother, child care for three children ate up what she could earn at her job. The familiar refrain is that society cannot "afford" minimal support for the poor, and trying to get what public assistance there is an endless humiliating bureaucratic hassle. "Helpful" individuals are likely to consider a poor woman fair game for cheap sex. The children of the poor come to school with untreated infections or other health problems and ill-fed after a poor night's sleep, from homes where books, magazines, trips, and other enrichment are just a dream. (They may then be obtusely labeled as lazy, having a poor attention span, being retarded, having a behavior problem, etc.) For people without a car, access to distant public health facilities is a nightmare, and hospital stays entail ghastly neglect of small children without someone to care for them. A sorry familiar story is that of the male running out on the family when unemployment and too many children get too much for him.

3. Parker keeps saying that the poor are polite—there is no indictment here of politicians, lobbyists, or the well-fed callous majority. Hers is a voice of despair, but a determined and eloquent voice all the same?

TALKING, LISTENING, WRITING

4. Somewhat of a rhetorical question. Drastic cuts in health, education, and welfare programs threaten to push many more Americans into the ranks of an unemployable poverty-stricken underclass.

5. Calls for "welfare reform" have echoed through recent election campaigns. What do they mean in practice?

6. Writers like Jonathan Kozol (*Rachel and Her Children*) have been effective spokespersons for the dispossessed.

PROJECTS

7. Parker says that social workers often "quit in defeat or despair." Is this still true today?

THINKING ABOUT CONNECTIONS

Where do your students position themselves on the spectrum that ranges from the conservative "it's their own fault" to the liberal "it reflects the failures of society"?

Student Essay

Paul Correa, "Stigmatizing the Immigrant"　　280

Legislation aimed at discouraging illegal immigration and curtailing legal immigration early became part of the backlash politics of the '90s. Correa is one of the many students and faculty who argued, protested, and demonstrated trying to stop the passage and implementation of anti-immigration initiatives. Other Western countries—France, Germany, England—are experiencing similar controversies and agonized rethinking of immigration and asylum policies.

THE RESPONSIVE READER

1. According to Correa, the official aim of the California initiative, Proposition 187, was to stem the flow of illegal immigration by denying undocumented aliens and their children educational and medical services, except in emergencies. Educators, doctors and medical personnel, social workers, and public officials would be required to report individuals suspected of being illegal aliens. Correa claims that the underlying motive is to try to reverse the shift in demographics that is making California a predominantly Mexican American (Latino) and Asian American (Chinese, Japanese, Vietnamese, Filipino) state. The initiative is the expression of a wave of anti-foreign sentiment and the revival of racial discrimination.

2. Federal laws and a Supreme Court decision prohibiting the barring of illegal immigrants' children from the schools are being ignored. Federal money aimed at promoting equal educational opportunity is being jeopardized. The resulting further fee increases in the colleges will

aggravate the trend of limiting access to college to the offspring of affluent whites.

3. The singling out of students of color as "suspect," the creation of a large mass of students denied education and health care through no fault of their own, the reckless disregard of the threat to public health for all citizens, and the criminalizing of large numbers of long-term residents are among the considerations that might sway readers with a social conscience.

TALKING, LISTENING, WRITING

4. Ask students to report on personal encounters with supporters and opponents of anti-immigration initiatives. You may want to arrange for a panel of students discussing the pros and cons.

5. Are your students familiar with the tradition and philosophy of civil disobedience? Do they think there is a "higher law" that supersedes unjust or shortsided current laws?

6. Allow for a candid expression of views.

PROJECTS

7. Not only a college administration but also various departments, advocacy groups, and student organizations are likely to publish newsletters and similar publications touching on current issues. There may be active and vocal local branches of organizations ranging from the AAUW to the NRA.

Short Story

Simon J. Ortiz, "Kaiser and the War"   283

Kaiser in this story is the archetypal outsider. He is unable to relate to and honor the mores and laws of a society of which he is not really a part, and he is in turn destroyed by it.

THE RESPONSIVE READER

1. Kaiser went to school for perhaps two grades and "didn't speak good English." However, he "was pretty good-looking and funny in the way he talked," encouraged his grandfather to keep telling "stories about the olden times" after the other kids fell asleep, and worked hard in the fields or at the sheep camp. Among the villagers, sentiment is divided between those who think Kaiser is crazy and those who are afraid of him. The narrator and his mother may be the only people who belong to neither camp.

2. A breakdown in communication is at the heart of this story? To begin with, the "law people" and the people in the village speak different languages; Kaiser's sister has to act as an interpreter. Faustin ignores the agent—and the agent concludes Faustin is a wise man at prayer. The interpreter says, "He is crazy," meaning Kaiser is crazy, and the sheriff yells back, "Who's crazy?" like a man "refuting an accusation." The sheriff reaches for his "six-shooter" when a meeting breaks up sooner than he wanted.

3. Society played a major part by having a war and insisting that Kaiser participate. Given what society had done heretofore to Kaiser's people, it is at best unrealistic to assume Kaiser would be eager to join the U.S. Army?

TALKING, LISTENING, WRITING

4. Is our sense of justice necessarily conditioned by our allegiance to our society and its institutions? Or is there a higher moral law that would require us to judge Kaiser from a less culture-bound perspective?

5. Note that in recent years, initiatives by concerned individuals as well as well-orchestrated media campaigns have often led to a reexamination or reversal of judicial decisions.

6. Differences between cultural assumptions may be graphically illustrated when groups like Buddhists, Sikhs, or Muslims become part of a community. Authors such as E. M. Forster in *A Passage to India,* Joseph Conrad in *Heart of Darkness,* and Chinua Achebe in *Things Fall Apart* have explored the barriers to communication in the meeting of different cultures.

7. What is the difference between breaking the law and rebelling against the law?

PROJECTS

8. Have your students had first-hand experience with Americans living on the margins of our society?

Poem

Walt Whitman, "A Glimpse"   293

This poem is not so much about "sexual orientation" as about a way of relating to other human beings in defiance of a bigoted society.

THE RESPONSIVE READER

1. While society at large has often stereotyped the homosexual life as "revolting" and "disgusting" (Senator Jesse Helms), in this poem the

straight crowd is noisy and given to drunken oath and "smutty jest." The two gay men, by contrast, are quiet and sensitive, "happy in being together." The two lovers share a quiet moment and a tenderness that is likely to escape the noisy heterosexual crowd.

2. Recognizing that this poem is not so much about sex as about love might be a first step.

3. Readers who have stereotyped Whitman as the extrovert rhapsodic bard will have to find a more subdued, sensitive register for this poem?

TALKING, LISTENING, WRITING

4. Gay members of Congress, judges, and ministers as well as entertainers or musicians have gone public or been "outed" in recent years.

5. Is this a skinhead phenomenon? Is it a small-town or back-country phenomenon? What is the role of fundamentalist religion?

CHAPTER 6

IDENTITY: Gender and Race   303

Of the forces that help shape our identity, how much is biology, how much is cultural conditioning, and how much is individual choice? Americans today no longer simply accept the roles that accidents of birth and social status seem to have charted for them. They ask questions like the following: When we define gender roles, how much is programmed by biology, and how much is age-old conventions of patriarchal societies? What does it mean to be black or Asian in white America? What kind of self-assertion and protections should gays and lesbians strive for to be able to live fulfilled lives in a traditionally homophobic society? Many of the essays in this chapter develop a vital contrast between then and now. They thus provide models and topics for writing assignments asking students to develop a purposeful comparison and contrast of past and present or ideal and reality.

Zora Neale Hurston, "How It Feels to Be Colored Me"   305

"Through it all I remain myself," Zora Neale Hurston asserts in this essay, sounding like a person determined to be less bedeviled by the demons of racism than most.

THE RESPONSIVE READER

1. Hurston's self-esteem seems a defiant assertion of self-worth in the face of a society whose meannesses and exclusions she knew as well as anybody. She asserts that "the world is to the strong regardless of a little pigmentation more or less," and she clearly intends to be one of the strong. Hurston views the grim history of slavery as part of her preparation for the race of life. "The world is to be won and nothing to be lost." Sometimes when Hurston walks down Seventh Avenue, "The cosmic Zora emerges. I belong to no race nor time. I am the eternal feminine with its string of beads." Comfortable within herself, Hurston views her past as a challenge and sees the present as a world of possibility.

2. When she was thirteen, Hurston left "the little Negro town of Eatonville" and went to school in Jacksonville, and it was at this time she realized she "was now a little colored girl." Before this she was aware that white people did not live in her town. She distances herself from "Negrohood" by refusing to believe nature gave blacks "a lowdown dirty deal" and by refusing to feel defeated by the history of slavery. She is most aware of racial differences at mainly white Barnard College and while listening to jazz with a white friend, whose reactions to the music are conspicuously less joyful than Hurston's are. However, "I do not always feel colored," Hurston says, and, "At certain times I have no race, I am me."

3. Hurston's last word on race is that she has "no separate feeling about being an American citizen and colored." When she feels discriminated against, Hurston is astonished rather than angry: "How can any deny themselves the pleasure of my company!"

TALKING, LISTENING, WRITING

4. Hurston may be seen as a precursor of the current movement toward pride and self-assertion, although an essential part of her strategy is to downplay racial difference. What is missing is the militancy and adversarial stance toward the white power structure often found today?

5. Validating the history, art, and music of minority groups is a familiar avenue for restoring pride in racial or ethnic identity.

6. Reading the professional literature, one might conclude that feelings of inadequacy and low self-esteem are endemic among adolescents, women, school dropouts, workers in repetitive or little-valued jobs, and so on.

PROJECTS

7. Collaborative planning and implementation of a festival of ethnic or minority art or music (or ethnic food) may provide opportunities for instructive group work.

THINKING ABOUT CONNECTIONS

Pride and self-reliance are a common thread, with more open defiance of institutionalized white racism in Maya Angelou's "Step Forward in the Car, Please."

Patty Fisher, "The Injustice System: Women Have Begun to Fight"   310

Because they see our justice system as actually "The Injustice System" when it confronts rape, spouse abuse, and sexual harassment, women, according to Patty Fisher, are beginning to incline to "vigilante justice."

THE RESPONSIVE READER

1. Since the justice system has long been dominated by men, it has been the tendency to challenge or discredit a woman's allegations and to believe a man's denial. Fisher quotes an FBI estimate that only one in ten rapes is reported—in part, she assumes, because the victim assumes that the courts will believe the man.

2. Fisher challenges entrenched attitudes by an imaginary scenario placing a male victim of a gunpoint robbery in a situation analogous to the procedure a rape victim endures. His motives, reactions, attire, are all questioned and challenged, and without witnesses, the jury rules against him.

3. Fisher observes: "It's hard to change 3,000 years of attitudes." Historically women "were regarded as the property of first their fathers and then their husbands." Wife beating until the 1800s was not a crime. "There was no such thing as rape of a married woman" since she was supposed to fight to the death to protect her "husband's good name." The definition of "consent" has been muddied because parents for generations taught "that only bad girls have sexual feelings." Consequently, "'no' sometimes meant 'yes,'" so girls could "feign resistance," remain "good girls," and experiment with sex "without taking responsibility for it."

4. In future girls should be taught to defend themselves, to say and mean "no" or "yes," to realize the system can be unjust, and to "work to reform" an unjust system. Fisher is not advocating retribution killing, but she is acknowledging that "vigilante justice" is sometimes "the only way" that justice will be done—as in the case of the media exposure of previously shielded public officials, whose career may be terminated with "no criminal charges, no trial, no witnesses."

TALKING, LISTENING, WRITING

5. Given the number of women who are assaulted and raped in the United States, most students will have observed or heard something on the subject. (Remember that the subject may be too painful for open discussion or writing.)

6. Traditionally, men (including male judges, not to mention defense lawyers) have tended to have different ideas from women on who is "to blame?"

7. Try to make sure that students at some point in the course do one of these "walk-a-mile-in-my-shoes" assignments.

8. Would a mother and a father write similar letters? How different would be a letter sent to a daughter from one sent to a son?

PROJECTS

In recent years, the sensational Mike Tyson and William Kennedy Smith cases have tested attitudes (and produced very different legal outcomes).

THINKING ABOUT CONNECTIONS

Students should note that the justice system here comes in for severe criticism from both those accused of crime and the victims of crime who feel that justice is not done.

Naomi Wolf, one of the most successful and widely published women journalists, deplores the dearth of women commentators on topics other than "women's issues." Despite the explosion of talk and print on the information superhighway, there is one area of profound silence. What is that profound silence? "It is the sound of women not talking."

THE RESPONSIVE READER

1. To show that women are largely excluded from the marketplace of opinion, Wolf does some counting amongst the "elite media." In a year, one television talk show presented 55 female guests and 440 male guests. A month's sample of two national newspapers reveals that women were responsible for writing approximately fifteen percent of the editorial pieces published. Female contributors in a year's worth of magazines are counted, as are the female bylines in other publications. Talk show radio hosts who are women number 50 out of a total of 900. All of Wolf's statistics point to "passive but institutionalized discrimination on the part of editors and producers."

2. To the charge that women's writing tends to be too personal and emotional, Wolf replies that the charge has "some merit" but that "a double standard is at work here." Women are not alone in introducing the personal and emotional, but when men do the same, such "discussion is perceived as being central and public." Wolf claims that the question of homosexuals in the military, "the nationalism of German skinheads, the high melodrama of the World Cup and the recent convulsion of Japan-bashing" are essentially an international and on-going therapy session "on vulnerability and self-esteem conducted primarily by men about men." Indeed, "one could read the Western canon itself as a record of men's deep feelings of alternating hope and self-doubt." Wolf concludes that both men and women writers draw on personal feelings, the only difference being that "the author's maleness will elevate the language as being importantly public, while the author's femaleness stigmatizes it as being worthlessly private."

3. Both extremes of female punditry are "conditions of constraint." Choosing the "female perspective" because it is "one realm over which they can claim authority" means that two constraints will come into effect. If everything is to be approached from the female perspective, the field of what is available or of interest is considerably narrowed. At the same time, women writers are forced to shoulder "a heroic but cumbersome burden. They are forced, by the relative paucity of female pundits at the highest levels, to speak 'for women' rather than simply hashing out the issues in a solitary way." The opposite "no-uterus" extreme forces a woman writer to disavow anything pertaining to women. It "gives a publication the benefit of a woman's name on the title page, without the mess and disruption of women's issues entering that precious space."

4. Editors of some of the nation's most prestigious magazines told Wolf: "Women simply do not submit articles in the same numbers that men do." A count of unsolicited manuscripts received by a national paper and national newsmagazine indicates that men, at an absolute minimum, submit twice as many unsolicited manuscripts as women, and in some cases they submit ten times as many manuscripts as women. Since women are achieving parity with men "at the middle ranks of the law and the academy" and since women write as well as men, this reluctance to participate may be a response to subliminal signals from the culture at large. These signals may discourage women from assertiveness, frankness, and argumentativeness.

5. Wolf asserts that the traits "required by writing opinion journalism or appearing on adversarial public affairs shows are often in conflict with what are deemed 'appropriate' female speech patterns and behavior." She quotes the linguist Deborah Tannen, who says that "women and men often speak in different ways—women seek intimacy and consensus," while men "seek status and independence." Tannen also observes that conflict, which is the essence of public opinion writing and talk show arguments, is something that boys are raised to view "as a way to express bonding, while girls are raised to avoid conflict in their play and enforce consensus." Two psychologists are quoted who note that women are more "relational" and men are more "autonomous." As Wolf sums up: "Unfortunately, you can't write strong, assertive prose if you are too anxious about preserving consensus; you can't have a vigorous debate if you are paralyzed with concern about wounding the sensitivities of your opposite number." ("Solipsism," combining the two Latin words for "alone" and "self," is a philosophical theory that holds that one can know nothing except one's own experiences and conditions, and that one's self is the only thing that exists or is real.)

6. In the nineties, Hilary Rodham Clinton is experiencing the same sort of criticism and marginalization that Eleanor Roosevelt experienced in the thirties and forties. This is a trend that existed well before Cleopatra was vilified and will continue well after Margaret Thatcher ceases to inspire vitriol.

TALKING, LISTENING, WRITING

7. You may want to send students out for interviews or stage a panel discussion of women students to elicit candid responses to these questions.

8. You may ask students to compile a scrapbook of material from recent issues to help substantiate their findings.

9. Encourage the expression of a range of perspectives on this basic question of strategy and personal commitment.

PROJECTS

10. Ask students familiar with the charting of group dynamics to take the lead here.

Joe Gutierrez, "On the Job"   327

Joe Gutierrez is a working-class American to whom race issues are not theory but part of everyday living at work and in his neighborhood.

THE RESPONSIVE READER

1. For Gutierrez, group identity or group loyalty was not automatic. Because he did not "look" Mexican and did not speak Spanish, he was "not accepted by the Mexicans." He "forced" himself to learn Spanish in order to "get by." Gutierrez was raised in a non-racist environment and first became conscious of racism when he took a black child with him to a public swimming pool in East Chicago, causing white swimmers to flee the pool and close it down. His environment was a neighborhood mixed with Puerto Ricans and blacks, and, in consequence, Gutierrez learned to judge a person by criteria other than skin color. In turn, Gutierrez desires to be judged the same way himself, not as a member of one race or another, but as a human being. (Increasingly, he sees people segregating themselves on the basis of racial or ethnic identity in the same neighborhood or the same street.)

2. Gutierrez sees more racist attitudes in society at large than in the workplace, where, he claims, the job has to be done regardless of the prejudices of the people involved. He remembers times and places when Mexicans were treated the same as blacks. He does not see much racial tension at work but finds decisions are increasingly made solely on the basis of race and have nothing to do with merit or qualification. He tries to convince fellow Mexicans that if they use the racial slurs used by whites they imitate people who would use similar ugly language about them: "If a white guy says nigger . . . I bet he calls you spic."

3. Gutierrez has worked in Chicago's steel mills and has seen the changing role of race in company policy, in union elections, and in relations with his fellow workers. In union elections today, the majority of workers follow group loyalty and vote for someone of their own ethnic group or race, even if their candidate is noticeably less qualified than someone else. For a long time, racial discrimination prevailed. The steel mills assigned jobs on the basis of race: "Whites ran the trains, Latins worked on the tracks, and blacks worked in the coke plants." In 1977, however, the federal government stepped in and forced the plant to discontinue and make amends for such discrimination. To some extent now the shoe seems to be on the other foot: Blacks with a strong sense of grievance band together and make demands designed to compensate for past injustices. As he sees it, the company— Inland Steel is not racist or nonracist—but cares strictly about profit. Gutierrez says, "I don't think the company is racist. That's too simple. It's the bottom line, the dollar." Workers mean nothing to the company, and the race of workers is even less important.

4. Gutierrez' honesty comes through, for instance, when he describes the racism of groups, when he describes the younger blacks who came into the mill with an active sense of grievance twelve to fifteen years ago, and when he admits that he, too, used to vote for all candidates with Hispanic names rather than for the most qualified.

TALKING, LISTENING, WRITING

5. Gutierrez is an old-style union member trying to adjust to working in an integrated but declining industry—giving many readers a glimpse of a working-class world different from the world of school or office.

6. Gutierrez makes us see and think about conflicting loyalties and cross currents that get lost in the great polemical confrontations?

7. Gutierrez dates back to the industrial America of an earlier time, and he has seen and sympathized with the changes brought about by the politics of racial equality. Many of today's Americans no longer share his loyalties and perspective?

8. Gutierrez' ability to see the other side in race issues and his patient commonsensical attempts to be a force for good are encouraging—but we also need to remember that he was sought out by an editor known for his liberalism and good will?

PROJECTS

9. Your students may want to focus on recent reports and surveys that would tend to confirm or update these data.

Shelby Steele, "White Guilt"   332

"White Guilt" is one of several essays in which Steele probed the psychology of racism, diagnosing the psychological mechanisms that make both perpetrator and victim play their foreordained parts. Steele was embraced by conservatives who interpreted his criticism of affirmative action as an endorsement of callous inaction. He was violently attacked by members of the black community who saw him as undermining desperately needed government programs at a time of retrenchment and cynicism. Few, however, could quarrel with his basic premise that decades of civil rights legislation and affirmative action policies had left large numbers of African Americans without direction, motivation, or hope.

THE RESPONSIVE READER

1. Steele posits a major change in white attitudes toward race as the crude overt racism of earlier years gave way to official soul-searching and

breast-beating. In a typical situation of the 1950s, Steele listened to the cowardly anguish of a caddymaster who enforced the racist policies of a country club. By the 1960s, "the absorption of another's cowardice was no longer necessary." "The lines of moral power, like plates in the earth," has shifted as the result of the civil rights movement and the black-power movement. The symbolic significance of the civil rights legislation is that it was "an admission of white guilt," and with this legislation, the nation "acknowledged its fallenness, its lack of racial innocence." In regards to race, like Adam and Eve after the Fall, the nation developed a consciousness of sin, acknowledging that it had "rationalized for many years a flagrant injustice."

2. The facts that twenty years later "the gap between blacks and whites is widening rather than narrowing" and "segregation is more entrenched in American cities" are to Steele evidence that the promises of the civil rights era have not materialized. Public policy took the wrong turn when it embraced a social policy bent on expiating past wrongs rather than "the much harder and more mundane work of black uplift and development."

3. The story of the restroom tip confirms Steele's view of the workings of white guilt. The businessman was forced to acknowledge "his ill-gotten advantage as a white." This made him feel guilty, and the guilt made the businessman feel two things: first, he wanted to redeem his innocence, and second he "wanted to escape the guilt-inducing situation." The businessman thus bought his escape and a sense of redemption (authentic redemption would occur if "the source of our guilt" were confronted) with his twenty-dollar tip. The nation as a whole acts out the same scenario on a larger scale: Black entitlement programs, "offering more than fairness," are, among other things, the nation's attempt to exorcise its guilty conscience and to push the situation out of mind.

4. Black militants acted as the author's friend did with the businessman: they forced the nation to confront its guilt. Militancy activates "the kind of white guilt in which whites fear for their own decency and innocence." The nation's guilty conscience allows it to be pressured for "reparation and compensation for past injustice."

5. According to Steele, racial preferences have had "the same effect as racism" because blacks are treated as "a separate species for whom normal standards and values do not automatically apply."

TALKING, LISTENING, WRITING

6. Charges of reverse discrimination and vocal attacks on a "quota system" have been an effective part of the backlash against affirmative action. College admission and especially also admission to law schools and medical schools as well as financial aid programs are affected by changes in official policies on these points, impinging upon the fortunes of many. Have students had experience with tutorial programs or other special programs for minority students?

7. Steele says that he never writes about anything that he has not himself experienced. At the same time, his careful scholarly analyses seem removed from the raw hostility and despair of many inner-city blacks?

8. Attempts to integrate city schools and similar tests of attitudes toward race may be of recent enough memory for students to examine changing attitudes and assumptions.

PROJECTS

9. Students are likely to encounter a range of vocal opinions on this subject.

Randall E. Majors, "America's Emerging Gay Culture"   340

In recent years, an extensive literature has developed examining the lives of famous homosexuals, gay relationships, gay politics, images of gays in the media, the gay lifestyle, and the problems of young gay people. Majors' essay is part of a general movement toward defining positive self-images for members of the gay community. Majors says "the relative differences and similarities between gay men and lesbians is a hotly debated issue in the gay/lesbian community," but for the purpose of this article he chose to speak of them as a single unit.

THE RESPONSIVE READER

1. The gay neighborhood is a "special place that is somehow imbued with 'gayness'" and reinforces a gay person's sense of identity. The area is "hospitable to the group's unique values." Such a neighborhood develops when gays reside there, when word spreads that "a certain area is starting to look attractive and open to gay members," when enough clientele moves into the area and gay businesses ("operated by or catering to gay people") develop, and when "social groups and services emerge." Friendships are particularly critical because gays are often isolated by homophobia. In larger cities there exists a wide range of social groups that "add to the substance of a gay culture." Gay bars serve as a "central focus" despite the liabilities of age requirements, alcoholism, and AIDS.

2. Symbols permeate gay culture, particularly as it moves from private "personal experience" toward becoming a "public phenomenon." For instance, names of establishments catering to gays used to use code words like *blue* or *other* and are now moving to "hypermasculine referents" such as *studs* and *boots,* while lesbians tend to prefer the use of personal names or classical allusions (Artemis). Keys worn on belts or colored handkerchiefs give coded signals to the initiated. Representations of gays in the media "are stereotypes that often oversimplify gay people . . . and do not discriminate the subtleties of human variety in gay culture." The media are slowly working

toward a more supportive view of a gay lifestyle as "American culture gradually becomes more accepting of and tolerant toward gay people."

3. Majors says that the movement toward political influence and toward a positive self-identity on the part of gays has taken place "often under repressive and sometimes dangerous conditions." The creation of gay social groups is partly a result of homophobia. Because gays are rejected by others or are afraid of being discovered, gay social groups are created. Their function in part is to help gay people find other gays so that their needs for affiliation and human contact can be met, shielded from a homophobic society.

4. Majors questions the common stereotype that gay men used "exaggerated, dramatic, and effeminate body language—the 'limp wrist' image." He also discusses the stereotypes of "cross-gender dressing, known as 'drag,' and a specialized, sexually aggressive argot called 'camp.'" As a result of gay liberation, no stereotypical behavior would adequately describe gay communication styles in the 1990s.

TALKING, LISTENING, WRITING

5. Students will see similarities, although perhaps gays strive harder for "home turf" in response to the larger society's persecution of their lifestyle. But at the same time they seem less subject to the "territorial imperative" that aggressively drives out outsiders.

6. Such movements generally aim at both legal protections and changes in public attitudes, particularly as reflected in the media? They also experience successes and periods of backlash as society at large moves toward more liberal or more conservative ideas.

7. In some areas (Oregon, Colorado), homophobic initiatives have fueled much controversy and attracted extensive media attention. AIDS research has come under attack in the U.S. Congress by homophobic legislators.

PROJECTS

8. The unequivocal repudiation of anti-gay policies in the military that many had hoped for did not materialize, with new policies in place that many find contradictory and that are still in flux?

Maxine Hong Kingston, "The Woman Warrior"   349

Maxine Hong Kingston claims that being a girl and being a bad girl were indistinguishable for her parents and her family. In her journey to a sense of self-worth, she had to slay the twin dragons of sexism and racism. She is a powerful writer who chronicles the pain and confusion of a young Chinese woman growing up in America while being haunted by China and its past.

THE RESPONSIVE READER

1. Sayings that Kingston's family brought from their native village help perpetuate the extreme misogyny of traditional Chinese society: "Feeding girls is feeding cowbirds," "There's no profit in raising girls," "Better to raise geese than girls," "When fishing for treasures in the flood, be careful not to pull in girls." (Kingston claims that a Chinese word a female speaker uses to refer to herself is "slave.") Great-uncle roars "No girls!" and takes the boys for an exciting day in Chinatown, and the mother responds to a report of straight A's with a story about a girl who saves her village. Hardly surprising are Kingston's hostile reactions: "I would thrash on the floor and scream so hard I couldn't talk." She engages in furtive rebellions: "At my great-uncle's funeral I secretly tested out feeling glad that he was dead." She rebels against the stereotypically feminine chores: "When I had to wash dishes, I would crack one or two."

2. Kingston grew up in an extremely patriarchal society where boys were treasured and girls devalued. Tradition had it that "when you raise girls, you're raising children for strangers," since "females desert families." By contrasting the treatment afforded to her much-anticipated younger brothers, Kingston shows the deprivation girls endured. She imagined herself as a "warrior woman" avenging the wrongs suffered by her gender. As an adult, Kingston realized she "had to get out of hating range," so she does not live near family or emigrant villagers. She has the satisfaction of her "American successes" and has used her reporting as revenge and exorcism.

3. Racism in American society compounded the rebellious spirit engendered by a sexist upbringing. Kingston went into a different world at work, but she was still treated as an inferior. A bigoted employer squelched her feeble attempts to speak up for CORE or the NAACP. Urban renewal wiped out her family's laundry and their slum dwelling. In her fantasy world of fairy-tale and myth, the enemies are "business-suited in their modern American executive guise."

4. As regards the fate of her relatives in revolutionary China, Kingston seems in turn aggressive and resigned. She would like "to storm across China to take back our farm from the Communists" but she knows she is powerless. Perhaps the spirits are "resting happily in China" despite the brutal punishments meted out to people who were declared the class enemy.

5. Kingston makes use of the legend of the sword and creates a personal fantasy of the swordswoman who has forged a sword from her hatred of the injustice of her life. She resolves to be like a warrior in order to surmount life's obstacles.

TALKING, LISTENING, WRITING

6. Married American women have traditionally maintained much closer ties with their original families? The sentimentalizing of little girls, the tradition of "chivalry" and of putting women "on a pedestal," and the "beauty myth" help to disguise the American version of patriarchy?

77

7. Male students may exhibit various degrees of empathy.

8. Racism and sexism are often linked in current discussions as proceeding from a very similar mindset. (Shirley Chisholm once said that she would rather be black than a woman.)

9. We live in a society that has to a large extent learned to turn a deaf ear. What does it take to break through the crust of apathy?

PROJECTS

10. Footbinding in China was practiced because small feet on females were considered beautiful, and binding was the excruciating technique used to retard growth (and to help immobilize and confine women). Joan of Arc (approximately 1412–1431) was a medieval French saint and "woman warrior" who helped the French gain victory over the English and helped crown the future Charles VII of France during the 100 Years War. She was captured by the enemy and burned at the stake for heresy and witchcraft. Tongs were secret societies or fraternal organizations formed by Chinese living in the United States. The martial arts are typically weaponless forms of self defense. They were developed in China, India, and Tibet, and include jujitsu, judo, and karate. Ideographs are pictures or symbols used in a non-alphabetical system of writing. CORE is the Congress of Racial Equality, which was founded in 1942. It sought to end discrimination through nonviolent direct action.

Short Story

Alice Walker, "Everyday Use"   356

Alice Walker says that during the civil rights movement of the sixties she was "young and bursting with fear and determination to change our world." One editor said that a theme of much of her work was her "admiration for the struggle of black women toward self-realization in a hostile environment."

THE RESPONSIVE READER

1. The mother is a heavy, hard-working, unsqueamish, and clear-eyed countrywoman suspicious of daydreams and refined airs. Her daydreams, like those of most Americans, are heavily colored by the media world of glitz, limousines, wisecracking emcees, and vibrant model families, but she never loses touch with the world as it really exists. She has a strong loyalty to family and a lively sense of family history.

2. The fire in which Maggie was badly burned is a recurrent symbol and plays a central role in the sisters' history. Dee is "lighter than Maggie, with

nicer hair and a fuller figure," and the physical disparity between the girls is exacerbated by Maggie's scars from the fire. Dee was sent away to school, while Maggie "knows she is not bright." Dee has embraced the "new day" in African American history at the cost of condescending to her family roots. Maggie enjoys sitting outside with her mother and chewing on a bit of snuff. Maggie is shy, retiring, and has no doubt never hurt a living thing, while Dee exhibits impressive "fault-finding power." "Hesitation was no part" of Dee's nature. During the fire Maggie was terrified and hurt. Dee, on the other hand, stood watching from under a tree, almost willing the complete destruction of the house she hated.

3. Dee and her companion represent the awakening black consciousness of an educated younger generation. They cast off names that remind them of "the people who oppress" them and seek to celebrate the things associated with their own culture. Dee makes certain her mother's house appears in all her Polaroids, cherishes the benches "her daddy made for the table," and wants to use the worn churn top "as a centerpiece for the alcove table." Rather than putting the artifacts of their culture to everyday use, Dee and her companion seek to display them. The culture is thus transformed from a living thing to a museum piece? Their talk, even when communicating with their downhome family, is emphatically educated, refined, and free of slang.

4. Dee wants the quilts to be displayed as symbols of her heritage—but the quilts have been promised as a wedding present to Maggie, who will put them to "everyday use." This specific conflict is a replay of a lifelong pattern in which Dee made her demands and shy Maggie acceded. The quilts were made of "pieces of dresses Grandma used to wear" (ironically Grandma Dee, whose name Dee has shed) and are symbolic of the family's endurance, talent, and struggle with poverty. The ending resolves the conflict by revealing to the mother the stellar qualities embodied by Maggie. In a moment of epiphany, the mother hugs Maggie, "something she had never done before," and returns the quilts to her.

TALKING, LISTENING, WRITING

5. Although the story seems stacked against Dee, some students may sympathize with the impulse to leave the rural past behind.

PROJECTS

6. Use this project as an opportunity to bring the students' own imagination and creativity into play.

Judy Grahn, "Nadine, Resting on Her Neighbor's Stoop" 365

The poet here shows herself to be totally emancipated from the "beauty myth" and traditional feminine stereotypes as she pays tribute to a tough and strong "common woman."

THE RESPONSIVE READER

1. A woman spiking drinks at Sunday socials, a woman from "a mud-chinked cabin in the slums," a woman made of "grease / and metal, with a hard head," a woman reminiscent of an "armored tank"—these are some of the striking images and details Grahn uses for her portrait of Nadine.

2. The poem is meant as a tribute to the countless "common women" who do not populate the pages of *Vogue* or *Elle* and without whose work and moral strength their neighborhood or their family would "burn itself out."

3. If the traditional "feminine image" envisions a dainty weaker sex, Nadine is very unfeminine. A traditional female would not collect bail, spike drinks, see herself as a "ripsaw," have "big hands," count rats, and make "the men around her seem frail."

TALKING, LISTENING, WRITING

4. Images of women like Nadine may occasionally surface in "slice-of-life" movies or television programs—but the housewife gushing about cleaner dishes and shirts (in advertising) and the hooker or screaming victim of a sadistic killer (on the tube) seem by far more common?

5. In some ethnic traditions, the strong matriarchal woman—mother, grandmother, or aunt—was a familiar part of family life?

PROJECTS

6. For instance, late-at-night addicts of sitcom reruns should be able to show that Mary Richards (*The Mary Tyler Moore Show*), a television news producer who is happily single, is a far cry from Laura Petrie (*The Dick Van Dyke Show*), stay-at-home wife and mother. Yet many of Mary's dealings are with a male boss and with male coworkers whom she humors or works her way around. What more recent sitcoms center on a female boss humored by male workers?

THINKING ABOUT CONNECTIONS

Choices may range from Irving Stone's pioneer woman to Maxine Hong Kingston or the mother in Alice Walker's "Everyday Use."

CHAPTER 7

MEDIA WATCH: Image and Reality   375

The perceived reality of many Americans is shaped or influenced in basic ways by the media. Students spend more time on television viewing than on schoolwork. For every voter who has seen a live presidential or senatorial candidate on a college campus, there are a hundred others who have seen the candidate only in images tailored, formatted, or orchestrated by the media. This chapter brings together writers exploring key ingredients in the mix of information, entertainment, and advocacy that the mass media serve up twenty-four hours a day. The media thrive on "hot topics" and the exploitation of genuine or fake issues. They tend to become embroiled in controversies over censorship and access as factions battle for representation of their views. These essays therefore provide models and topics for papers playing off the pro and con—the "one-two" of statement and counterstatement that is the antidote to blinkered, self-righteous views.

Patricia Jacobus, "Boy Killed After School"   377

Like many news reports about routine violence on our streets and in our schools, this example of everyday journalism tries hard to report the unspeakable and obscene (the frivolous killing of a fifteen-year-old boy) in rational and objective language.

THE RESPONSIVE READER

1. One block away from American High School, on a Tuesday just before three in the afternoon, fifteen-year-old Alejandro Cueva was stabbed to death. Cueva had been walking with his friend, Alejandro Campos, who received a superficial stab wound. The pair were attacked by three other juveniles: "a 16-year-old former student, a 17-year-old runaway who had stopped attending classes, and a 16-year-old student." One of these three held Cueva's arms back and "another plunged a knife into his heart"; Cueva subsequently "collapsed to his death between two minivans on a car dealership's lot." The three youths were stopped initially "three blocks from the scene," but released; later the trio was brought by their parents to the police, and "after they learned that one of the victims had died, they admitted to the stabbing, police said." "The stabbing apparently was in retaliation for a comment made during a first-period class Tuesday," and the intended victim (apparently neither Cueva nor Campos were targeted) "fled before the fight started." The three suspects are white, and Cueva was Mexican. Alejandro Cueva was the oldest of four children, enjoyed track and basketball, and, according to his thirteen-year-old sister, "always had a lot of problems at the school because the other students don't like Chicanos."

2. Statistics point toward a rise in violent crime committed by juveniles, often against other juveniles. Although the headline treats the incident as if it were a "normal occurrence," the report itself does not. By including statements like Campos "just happened to be walking with the boy who made the final comment" and the stabbing was a response to comments made "about a hickey" on a boy's neck, the reporter calls attention to the outrageous nature of this incident, without actually putting it into words. When the reporter juxtaposes the events of the school's Spirit Week with the death of a fifteen-year-old, she again subtly points out what a tragedy Cueva's death is. Cueva should have been getting ready for the homecoming dance and the homecoming football game, not dying on a car dealership lot.

3. The reporter's interpretation echoes the interpretation of the police sergeant; neither wishes to inflame the tragedy by interjecting the issue of a racially motivated murder. Only at the end of the article does the reporter note that "police are downplaying race as a possible motive in the stabbing." Again, the facts that the assailants were white, that Cueva and Campos were Mexican, and that Cueva had problems at the school because of prejudice and bigotry, are reported only at the end of the article. Another reporter might have placed these facts first in the article and produced a report that treated the event as racially motivated from the outset. Other interpretations of this incident could include more of a focus on juvenile violence or a more incendiary treatment of the race issue.

TALKING, LISTENING, WRITING

4. The fact that this incident arose over some verbal horseplay about hickeys (at least on the surface) and that Cueva was not even involved in the conversation makes it hard to describe such violence as anything but brainless and insane. One lesson to be learned might be that a concerted effort is needed to minimize slurs and hate speech in the schools. A less traditionally liberal approach might be to reexamine the policy of exposing the victim's family to the glare of sickening publicity while shielding the killers.

5. Perhaps some questionnaire involving current news stories could be devised to test the capacity of students to be shocked (or their tendency to be numbed) by routine homicidal violence.

6. If possible, arrange informal publication and sharing with the class of the results.

PROJECTS

7. Preparing a collage or compiling a chamber-of-horrors collection of relevant recent news reports might prove a sobering educational experience.

In this scathing indictment of current journalistic practices, one of the country's best-known journalists deplores the abandonment of the standards of investigative journalism. The distinction between tabloid journalism or yellow journalism and the *New York Times* or *Chicago Tribune* is being erased as rumor drives out carefully researched fact, as the drive to scoop the competition makes it impossible to verify information, and as the freakish and sleazy become the norm.

THE RESPONSIVE READER

1. Bernstein almost immediately says that "the America rendered today in the American media is illusionary and delusionary—disfigured, unreal, disconnected from the true context of our lives." According to Bernstein, "coverage is distorted by celebrity and the worship of celebrity; by the reduction of news to gossip, which is the lowest form of news; by sensationalism, which is always a turning away from a society's real condition; and by a political and social discourse that we—the press, the media, the politicians, and the people—are turning into a sewer." To be the first to break a major news story (and to receive advertising points for increased viewership or heightened readership) means that "speed and quantity substitute for thoroughness and quality, for accuracy and context." In such a "frenzied environment" and with such a "blizzard of information," serious analysis or follow-up is rendered obsolete.

2. Among Bernstein's examples to substantiate his indictment of the media are Diane Sawyer's prying question to Marla Maples (about the best sex); a New York primary election where serious news coverage was "eclipsed" by the sensationalism of talk radio, television talk shows, and the city's more tawdry newspapers; prestigious (or formerly so) newspapers like the *New York Times* naming a rape victim in a celebrity case and using a celebrity biographer on the front page; television's "Donahue-Geraldo-Oprah freak shows (cross-dressing in the marketplace; skinheads at your corner luncheonette; pop psychologists rhapsodizing over the airways about the minds of serial killers and sex offenders)"; and Ivana Trump, "perhaps the single greatest creation of the idiot culture, a tabloid artifact if ever there was one."

3. Trash and sleaze that used to exist on the fringes of the media have moved into the center. Bernstein says that the "great information conglomerates of this country are now in the trash business." Bernstein concedes that the "trash business" is protected by the First Amendment, but he laments that "we should always furnish it with an outlet." "There is hardly a major media company in America," he concludes "that has not dipped its toe into the social and political equivalent of the porn business in the last fifteen years." Trash journalism is replacing well-researched, well-written, and well-checked information; "never before have we had anything like today's situation in which supposedly serious people . . . live and die by (and

actually believe!) these columns and these shows and millions more rely upon them for their primary source of information."

4. You might want to ask your students to tape actual segments of talk shows for class discussion.

TALKING, LISTENING, WRITING

5. Coverage of the Michael Jackson marriage or of Madonna's exhibitionism are among earlier examples that students might investigate.

6. Public television stations often run documentary programs that report seriously on American life. Smaller circulation newsmagazines, like the one from which Bernstein's article was taken, aim at serious news analysis.

7. Ask students to present test cases or cases in point.

THINKING ABOUT CONNECTIONS

Naomi Wolf's article focuses on the dearth of women playing prominent roles in serious news analysis (on the *New York Times'* op-ed page, for instance). Carl Bernstein's focus is wider as it is a general critique of what ails American journalism today. Susan Jacoby's article is, like Wolf's, more narrowly focused ("I am a First Amendment junkie") on one aspect of American journalism, i.e., censorship. Bernstein's is the most pessimistic voice?

Gloria Naylor, "The Myth of the Matriarch"   385

In this famous discussion of a media stereotype, Gloria Naylor explains the history and persistence of the myth of the black matriarch. Despite the conflict between the myth and reality, the myth lives on "even among black women."

THE RESPONSIVE READER

1. The black matriarch as envisioned by the media is "alone, self-sufficient and liking it that way." She is portrayed as a tower of strength who holds the family together while imposing order with consummate self-assurance. The biblical patriarchs were the fathers of the human race, and the term continues to be used in various religions to designate a venerable leader. Through much of human history, the patriarch (literally a "ruling father" or fatherly ruler) was the head of the family or clan, handing on his rank or power to a son in the patrilinear fashion. A matriarchy is a group in which a female leader is the supreme head. In Greek myth, the Amazons were a matriarchal tribe of warlike women from Asia Minor. While

the Amazon women governed and fought, their men looked after the household chores.

2. Because black women were presumed to be "different from white women"—stronger and tougher—they had a contradictory role during slavery. On the one hand, they "did the woman's work of bearing children and keeping house," while on the other hand, they did "a man's work" in the fields.

3. Myths are created "to serve a need," and the myth of the matriarch allowed the image of these "independent Amazons" to override the truth that society had forced them to be more than human by refusing to allow their men full participation in the benefits of the community. The fact that sixty percent of black households are headed by women supports the myth, but the reality is that the majority are struggling to raise their families with desperately limited resources.

4. "Throughout their history," Naylor says, "black women could depend upon their men." In the late nineteenth and early twentieth century, however, "it was easier to make black man the brunt of jokes than to address the inequities that kept decent employment from those who wanted to work." The myth of the matriarch helped to perpetuate this situation. Pushing the blame for chronic black unemployment onto the men rather than onto a society that often refused to hire black men has resulted in black women trying to compensate for the situation.

TALKING, LISTENING, WRITING

5. Some students, unfortunately, may draw their assumptions mainly from television and the movies?

6. Do students remember a mother, grandmother, or aunt who enjoyed special authority and respect in a family or clan? Do they remember a matriarchal businesswoman, mayor, principal, college president?

7. Antagonism toward abusive black males plays a major role in recent fiction by black women, such as Alice Walker's *The Color Purple*.

PROJECTS

8. Which of the predictable types listed here seem a matter of the past? Which are still operating (or have come back)? Are your students aware or resentful of other stereotypes not listed here?

Movie Review

Richard Corliss, "False Hoops"   390

Playing upon the expression "false hopes," Corliss studies the way the movie *Hoop Dreams* deflates the dream of many young minority athletes aspiring to make it to the National Basketball Association.

THE RESPONSIVE READER

1. Both William Gates and Arthur Agee are young African American men from the Chicago projects who receive "full or partial scholarships to suburban St. Joseph High School, which is a three-hour round trip and social light years away from home." At St. Joseph's, the two "can make poetry of a jump shot, but to them algebra looks like Chinese." They are isolated at the school because they are "hired guns," who are "set apart by their race and their athletic gift." To win the state championship for St. Joseph's appears to be the overriding concern of far too many adults who interact with these boys: "These kids must perform under pressures that would break most adults." As a result of this pressure, the paths of the two young men diverge. Arthur transfers to a local high school, "where he becomes a star player." (Arthur's mother, "the film's heroine," gets "the top grade" and graduates from a nurse's-assistant course.) William, on the other hand, remains at St. Joseph's, where he is pushed too hard by a coach who is still trying to compensate for not pushing NBA star Isiah Thomas hard enough when he was at the school. At the end of high school, "William is an old man with a damaged knee, a child to support and some rueful wisdom."

2. The institution, the coaches, and the fans were treating the two young men as commodities. They were at St. Joseph's to lead the school to the state championships; no mention is made whatsoever of any academic successes there. They are "hired guns" at the school. "It became more of a job," says William about playing basketball for the school, "than a game to play." When Arthur Agee goes to Marshall High because his parents cannot afford to pay St. Joseph's recently raised tuition, the school "refuses to release Arthur's records, thus threatening him with loss of a full school year." Pressure from the fans ("in basketball you get an A or an F—win or lose, period—and everyone's watching") is complemented by pressure from the coaches. ("The St. Joe coach can't afford to bring William along slowly." William departs the school with "a damaged knee.") William is discarded as damaged goods, and Arthur is hounded for unpaid debts.

TALKING, LISTENING, WRITING

3. Students are likely to be torn between the feeling that no one should be discouraged from dreaming "the impossible dream" and Corliss' sobering statistics. ("Even if he's one of the 50,000 or so high school phenoms in a year, his chances are only one in 2,000 that he will play NBA basketball.")

4. One possibility is to compare a highly stylized, romanticized portrayal of the inner city like *West Side Story* with a harshly realistic depiction like *Boyz 'N the Hood*.

PROJECTS

5. Many institutions have gone through soul-searching, rethinking, and legal challenges concerning their athletic programs.

Gloria Steinem, "Erotica and Pornography"   393

D. H. Lawrence once said that Western civilization was clinically insane on the subject of sex. In this essay, one of the country's leading feminists maps out a sane, civilized, humane view of sex and distinguishes sexual stimulation among equal, freely consenting partners from pornography.

THE RESPONSIVE READER

1. Steinem sides with a liberal modern view of sex, emancipated from the prohibitions and inhibitions of a repressive traditional sex morality. Sexuality has evolved from a strict procreative function to "a form of expression" that serves the human needs of "bonding, of giving and receiving pleasure, bridging differentness, discovering sameness, and communicating emotion." However, "fear of change" has prompted the religious right to repress "nonprocreative sex," and women must move toward a society where they control their own sexuality.

2. The key distinction between erotica and pornography is the difference between mutual, reciprocal sexual satisfaction and coerced, exploitative sex. "Erotica" present images of "a mutually pleasurable, sexual expression between people who have enough power to be there by positive choice." Pornography depicts "sex being used to reinforce some inequality," catering to the need for "violence, dominance, and conquest." Women must fight against the "pornographic vengeance against women's sexuality" and promote sex that is "pleasurable, empathetic," and free from fear.

3. Steinem sees the issue of the censorship of pornography in the larger context of current sexual politics. Because both erotica and pornography have separated sexuality from conception, "the current backlash against women's progress" views erotica and pornography as "equally 'shocking.'" This view is held by the religious right, which sees women's struggle "to decide our reproductive futures" as a threat to the patriarchal structure. This "religious visceral backlash has a secular" counterpart that attempts to apply "the 'natural' behavior of the animal world to humans." Both movements see the female's first and only destiny as that of bearing and raising children. Steinem links the traditional division of "wife or whore" with the prevailing attitudes: wives have many children and do not think of sex separately from procreation.

4. To judge from current trends in the media, it is more acceptable to show women as victims of brutal assaults than to show women as joyous participants in "pleasurable, empathetic" lovemaking?

5. The essay could prove persuasive for many taking the "I'm-not-a-feminist, but" stance?"

6. The courts have at various times, and with much shilly-shallying and inconclusiveness, attempted to draw the line?

7. Artistic nudes have often been equated with pornography—but just as often been defended on grounds like "aesthetic distance" and the shaping, controlling influence of form.

PROJECTS

8. Some legal background: In 1957 (Roth v. United States), the Supreme Court determined that obscenity is not protected by the First Amendment. In Miller v. California (1973) the Court set a new test for obscenity that was intended to eliminate pornography. The Miller decision has been modified by other decisions, i.e., private possession of obscenity is not a crime (Stanley v. Georgia, 1969); states can prohibit the interstate transport of obscene materials (United States v. Orita, 1973); and states can refuse to allow the reception of obscene material through the mail (United States v. Reidel, 1971).

SUGGESTIONS FOR LANGUAGE WORK

We often have a better sense of the full meaning and implications of key terms in an argument when we know something about their origin or history. How can etymological information help students understand terms like *evolutionary, primate, atavistic, autonomous, objectification, coercion, erotic, voyeur, sadism, masochism*?

Susan Jacoby, "Pornography and the First Amendment"   399

Susan Jacoby, self-described as a "First Amendment junkie," takes an uncompromising view of the need to uphold freedom of speech even when faced with severe provocation. She speaks for journalists, writers, and artists who fear the precedent of censorship justified by whatever societal need or noble cause.

THE RESPONSIVE READER

1. Jacoby raises the spectre of censorship, warning feminist advocates of censorship against allying themselves with the repressive reactionary right. Jacoby deplores the alliance between feminists who would deny First Amendment protection to pornography and "adversaries of the women's movement, including opponents of the equal rights amendment." In the opening sentence of the second paragraph, she describes herself as a "woman writer who believes . . . in an absolute interpretation of the First Amendment." The attempt to censor pornography implies that pornography represents "a greater threat to women than similarly repulsive exercises of free speech pose to other offended groups" (for instance, the spouting of neo-Nazi slogans in a predominantly Jewish neighborhood). Such selective application of constitutional protection results in a dangerous precedent, favors women at the expense of equally oppressed and offended groups, and does not distinguish between "the expression of ideas and conduct."

2. Jacoby enters into the thickets of definition, stressing the notorious difficulty of drawing the line: "Are all naked pictures of women obscene?" Censors will be as unable to agree as the Supreme Court has been, although the "equation of sex and violence . . . has fed the illusion that censorship of pornography can be conducted on a more rational basis than other types of censorship." Jacoby makes an apparent exception for child pornography: She claims it is different because it is an abuse of the power parents have over children. Parents do not have the "right to use their children to make pornographic movies," just as they cannot send their children "to work in coal mines."

3. Censorship arises from irrational preferences, is practiced by people "opposed to open discussion of issues," is the state's abandonment and renouncement of "the possibilities of democratic persuasion," and reflects our present tendency to "shift responsibility from individuals to institutions." Jacoby would shift the responsibility back to individuals and would have each of us practice self-censorship by refusing to view anything we deem pornographic. This solution would require us to exercise especial parental vigilance as well as control our apparently instinctive urge to tell others what they may or may not do.

TALKING, LISTENING, WRITING

4.–6. An aversion to censorship has long been a cornerstone of the American liberal tradition. Do special situations require special remedies? Are there exercises of "free speech" that are simply beyond the pale of civilized society?

7. Teachers' organizations and librarians' groups log the many instances of overt and indirect censorship that affect schools and students.

PROJECTS

8. Jacoby's example of the ACLU defending the rights of American Nazis to hold a march in a community with many survivors of Nazi atrocities is a case in point.

Satire

Andrea Freud Loewenstein, "Sister from Another Planet Probes the Soaps"   404

Loewenstein uses the familiar literary device of a visitor come from afar to take a wide-eyed fresh look at practices so familiar that we no longer notice how weird or laughable they are.

THE RESPONSIVE READER

1. The space visitor's letter to the professor contains a number of playful allusions to the concept of serious research. For instance, "the human species North Americanus Soapus" ("Soapoids," for short) is a play on the biological classification of species. Investigation has revealed the reason "soap" is used to describe these television programs. There is an "obsessional recurrence of the cleanliness theme in the 'commercials,' which occur at rhythmic intervals throughout the tapes." "Objects of worship," to which "ritualized hymns of thanksgiving and praise" are directed, include "toilet bowl cleaners and vaginal deodorants." The narrator's tone throughout is that of an earnest observer conducting clinical trials to refute or support assumptions and theses. Send-ups of science fiction include this reminder to the out-in-space professor: "I float at a right angle in the front row; last Thursday I was an iridescent green with ocher spots." The time parameters of the investigation are specified as "the Earthling year 1993." In the first few paragraphs of the report, the reader learns that the narrator has seventeen sensors and that the narrator's species is divided into more than "a mere two fixed gender groupings."

2. The soaps reflect our real-life appetite for sex and gossip, although here carried to laughable extremes. The soaps are perhaps more honest than we are in everyday life about feelings of resentment and rivalry? All the men and women observed "were hostile toward their own gender, whom they perceived as rivals in their never-ending fight to possess the opposite sex." What is sad and funny is the paradoxical blend of prurience and prudishness in the soaps: Despite the fact that sex "appears to be the Soapoids' overwhelming motivational force, the humans in my sample spent almost no time actually copulating." There is a tremendous build-up toward "copulation" that never happens. A hilarious example occurred when a male "prepared for intercourse by placing at least 20 floating water lilies containing small lit candles in a pool of water upon which floated an inflatable rubber raft, the intended scene of sexual activity."

3. The exposure of (often long past) sexual irregularities is a standard element in the scandal-mongering world of the soaps. A conniving marriage to an apparently unsuspecting man, nosing about to find "information to determine the date of conception," calling off a wedding because of a scandal—these are all grist for the mill.

4. The filtering out of social realities and the perpetuation of stereotypes make for a pervasive air of smarmy dishonesty. There is no overt racial disharmony in soapland, contrary to what the narrator had expected, based on the professor's lectures. "I am happy to inform you that no such oppression exists among modern-day Soapoids," the narrator reports. "All hues mix and converse on terms of perfect equality and goodwill and hold titles of equal symbolic significance." Ironically, however, "darker and lighter humanoids do not mate, and appear to have no desire to do so," nor do any of the darker females achieve the vaunted status of Controller, "perhaps because they lack the necessary icy blue eyes." Only two members of ethnic "subspecies" were identified: Saul (who "appears to be a eunuch") is a member "of the subspecies 'Jew'"; Maria belongs to "the subspecies 'Latina,'" given to passion and horses. As regards class difference, it does not exist in soapland. "As of now, all Soapoids inhabit spacious, carefully color-coordinated cubes, filled with plastic flowers and bright modular furniture." The narrator concludes that the pictures the professor had shown the class of "unsavory dwelling places" are "out of date."

5. The narrator had been led to expect ethnic diversity, racial oppression, and impoverished lower classes, none of which exist in soap operas. Feminism is another area where there is great discrepancy between appearance and reality. The narrator had expected to see women "join with one another toward a common goal." However, there are no feminists in the soaps; instead there is a lot of animalistic posturing over who gets the rights to the alpha male. "In fact," the narrator observes, "the females' most favored posture was the standoff, a highly aggressive position in which two women position themselves from one to two feet apart and emit such statements as 'I hated you the first time I saw you.'" Such posturing is accompanied by a lot of "crossing of the arms, curling of the lip, and advancing in a menacing manner." Feminism has had no impact in the soap opera world. It is a place where no one actually works at a job, and each Soapoid's total reservoir of energy is directed at perpetuating the stereotypes of his or her "subspecies."

TALKING, LISTENING, WRITING

6. Seen from one perspective, the soaps present a fumigated dream world: The Soapoids are "a matriarchal people whose lives drag out in long luxurious segments lived within color-coordinated cubes, and who relegate the more messy business of life to quick one-minute segments, thus freeing themselves for a stress-free, germ-free, moisture-controlled existence." Seen from another perspective, the soaps may be true to the human capacity for conniving, jealousy, antagonism, gossipmongering, and being obsessed with sex.

7. The soaps are relatively free of the mindless sadistic violence that is the bane of much American entertainment. Allow critics and defenders of American popular culture to have their say.

8. You may want to ask students to check out the kinds of humor drawn upon by the increasing number of female stand-up comedians seen on television comedy hours and the like.

PROJECTS

9. Have students work in small groups and have each group present their findings to the class.

Poem

Sharon Olds, "The Death of Marilyn Monroe"   410

The story of Marilyn Monroe—the ultimate media creation—acquired mythical dimensions as writers ranging from macho to feminists and lesbians probed the symbolism of her life and death.

THE RESPONSIVE READER

1. The coldness and heaviness of the body ("heavy as iron"), the open mouth and eyes, the dead arms tied to the sides, and the breasts "flattened by / gravity" are spooky details that the poet uses to give harsh immediacy to the scene.

2. These ambulance attendants are no doubt familiar with death, but it is impossible for them to pretend they are dealing with just another routine corpse as they lift onto the stretcher the legendary Marilyn Monroe. With the demise of the film star, the men are made grudgingly aware of the ethereal nature of youth, beauty, fame, and life. One man reacts with depression and impotence, another with sudden dissatisfaction with his job and family, and a third feels the transitory nature of all that exists as he stands in a bedroom doorway, listening to the mortal sound of a "woman breathing, just an ordinary / woman / breathing."

TALKING, LISTENING, WRITING

3. Celebrity biography is a flourishing trade, and its aim often seems to be to expose the tortured human being behind the public persona?

4. Students may argue that the blonde stereotype has become more subtle since the days of Monroe and Mansfield.

PROJECTS

5. The wide-ranging perspectives on Monroe result, among other things, from her obscure lower-class origins, her meteoric rise and decline as a mega international film star, her sexual allure stimulating subterranean strata of the American psyche, and Hollywood's blatant packaging of her. She was a contradiction—a sex symbol studying with Lee Strasberg—who married or conducted liaisons with famous or powerful men who failed the test.

CHAPTER 8

ROLE MODELS: In Search of Heroes   419

Ours is not an age of hero worship. Gossip and scandal-mongering are the stock-in-trade of not just sleazy marginal journalism but of the mainstream media as well. The exposure or humiliation of the powerful, rich, and famous is a favorite spectator sport. This chapter focuses on a range of Americans who have provided inspiration or guidance for people— and especially young people, whose latent idealism makes them look for role models in a cynical society. Many of the writers in this chapter present convictions that bring deep-seated commitments and basic assumptions into play. They thus provide models and topics for papers arguing from principle —building an argument on a basic premise or basic premises that the writer expects the reader to accept.

Arthur Ashe, "A Black Athlete Looks at Education"   421

Outstanding African American athletes are a highly visible elite of fantastically overpaid superstars. "A Black Athlete Looks at Education" is Arthur Ashe's unsentimental look at blacks and athletics. He concludes that, given the odds against athletic success, young blacks should concentrate on getting an education.

THE RESPONSIVE READER

1. Ashe's thesis appears in the opening sentence: "Blacks spend too much time on the playing fields and too little time in the libraries." It is echoed again in the penultimate paragraph: "We need to pull over, fill up at the library, and speed away to Congress and the Supreme Court." He supports his thesis with sobering statistics and examples: at the time he wrote, 3,170 positions total in the major sports (!), relatively small turnover, sports careers finished by age 35, career-ending injuries, and the "star system," where for each athlete earning millions there are six or seven others earning much smaller salaries.

2. Ashe observes that "our most widely recognized role models are athletes and entertainers" and that boxers have been for blacks the "greatest heroes of the century." Our society tends to glorify and coddle African Americans when they are "runnin'," "jumpin'," "singin'," or "dancin'." But the glorification of the black athlete is part of a legacy of racial discrimination: Athletics and entertainment were the only areas open to blacks because "racial and economic discrimination" closed off all others.

TALKING, LISTENING, WRITING

3. The glamour, fame, and fantasy incomes associated with sports and entertainment are powerful lures, and the long slow grind of education (with no guarantee of economic advancement) may well look drab in comparison?

4. Perhaps a white kid who has a poster of a black baseball player on the wall of his room is less likely to be a total bigot than others—an open and debatable question.

5. The Magic Johnson story is one of many cases in point.

PROJECTS

6. Certainly the great spectator sports have an unprecedented following. How much active participation in sports has been the result of the current fitness craze?

Jenny Lyn Bader, "Larger Than Life"   424

"We require a new pantheon," Jenny Lyn Bader says, and perhaps we should call it a pantheon of role models, rather than one of heroes. Heroes are creatures of a bipolar world split between good and evil, between just and unjust, between right and wrong; thus they "are no longer in style." What our less clearly polarized world needs is the quiet voice of reason and understanding from role models.

THE RESPONSIVE READER

1. Eleanor Roosevelt (1884–1962) was the wife of Franklin Delano Roosevelt and the niece of another president. She worked as a speaker, writer, and indefatigable international campaigner to improve the lot of impoverished and voiceless Americans, victims of the Depression. Joan of Arc (1412–1431) is a Roman Catholic saint and French national heroine. Although she was only a teenager, she was instrumental in crowning the French king Charles VII, who had been prevented from assuming the crown by the English invaders during the Hundred Years War. Joan of Arc was eventually captured, and turned over to the English, who subsequently turned her over to the ecclesiastical court at Rouen, where she was tried for heresy (she claimed direct communication with God and thus bypassed Church hierarchy) and burned at the stake. Susan B. Anthony (1820–1906) was a leader of the women's suffrage movement who worked for decades trying to secure the vote for women finally granted by the Nineteenth Amendment in 1920. Anthony campaigned for women's rights to control their property, their rights to wages, and their rights in relation to their husband and children. Helen Keller (1880–1968) was left mute, blind, and deaf at the age of two by illness. Keller's parents sought help, and through Alexander Graham Bell arranged for a teacher, Anne Sullivan, whose teaching and

encouragement eventually saw Keller a Radcliffe graduate. Subsequently, Keller worked as a writer and a lecturer, working constantly to raise funds for programs for the blind. Jane Fonda, who was born in 1937, is the daughter of one of America's archetypal male actors, Henry Fonda. She won an Academy Award for the movie *Klute* in 1971, but, more importantly, she transformed herself from an actress capitalizing on her looks and name (*Barbarella*) to an actor capable of serious and moving performances (*Julia*). She has been prominently associated with many social and political causes, among them opposition to the Vietnam War.

2. Marilyn Monroe and Elvis Presley are icons in our culture because they are instantly recognizable symbols inextricably linked to American cultural history. Monroe, who died in 1962, was the quintessential blonde sex goddess, paradoxically cultivating an air of dizzy innocence. Elvis Presley, who died in 1977, was the swivel-hipped, curled lipped, rock and roll pioneer with an air of farm-boy naiveté. Both Monroe and Presley call to mind an America still innocent enough to find overt sexuality disturbing. Heroes, Bader says, "overcome massive obstacles," "do the right thing while enduring attractive amounts of suffering," "tend to be self-employed," "sense the future," and "lead lives that make us question our own." Heroes, in short, "are our ideals, but not our friends." Beethoven is a hero, as is Helen Keller and Franklin Delano Roosevelt. Heroes "lack irony," and are currently out of fashion. Both icons and idols continue to be in style, and both possess irony. Icons lend a "sexy" dimension to heroes, but without the nobility. Idols do not have the "universally beloved" status of heroes.

3. The objects of Bader's childhood hero worship were associated with the American Revolution, like Thomas Jefferson, or were adventurers and explorers, like Christopher Columbus. She sang about the exploits of these heroes in kindergarten, and read about them in "a set of books known as the 'Meet' series: *Meet George Washington, Meet Andrew Jackson, Meet the Men Who Sailed the Seas,* and many more." Bader makes analogies between her own life and the life of Columbus, as told in the "Meet" series. "Standing up to the king and queen" was similar to standing up to one's parents. To a child "who had trouble trying new foods let alone seeking new land masses," Columbus' bravery in the face of the unknown is inspirational. As regards Franklin, Bader had "a special fondness" for the "statesman and eccentric inventor." Other heroes like Washington and Jefferson and Samuel Adams and John Hancock, as presented in the books, "were funny-looking, but lovable. They did outrageous things without asking for permission. They invented the pursuit of happiness." Bader manages to re-create her girlish enthusiasm, and even conveys her grade-school naiveté (did the pursuit of happiness not exist until Jefferson wrote it down?).

4. Bader's childhood heroes did not survive her high school experience: "it was no longer hip to look up to the paternalistic dead white males who launched our country, kept slaves and mistresses, and massacred native peoples." Americans "started feeling queasy about heroism" in the 1970s and 1980s. As "the twentieth century draws to a close, outstanding human beings are the casualties of the moment," just as "kings and queens got roughed up at the end of the eighteenth century," and "God took a beating at

the end of the nineteenth." "Jealousy journalism" played a role in the modern debunking of heroes by compensating for its own lack of heroism by attacking anyone who might claim heroic status. "Jealousy journalism" also lowered "heroism standards by idealizing just about everyone." The debunking of heroes (done by "the generations that preceded ours") was the "side effect of a complicated cultural surgery." In the move to "a positive direction— toward greater tolerance, openness, and realism," Bader's childhood heroes did not survive.

5. As opposed to heroes, role models "are admirable individuals who haven't given up their lives or livelihoods and may even have a few hang-ups." Unlike heroes, role models are not called upon for "excessive self-sacrifice" or "hunger strikes." Role models are not the offspring of gods; they are a fourth-grade teacher in Chicago or someone's ninety-year-old Polish great-grandmother. When Bader explains why our modern world is more receptive to role models, she makes a key point: "A world without heroes is a rigorous, demanding place, where things don't boil down to black and white but are rich with shades of gray; where faith in lofty, dead personages can be replaced by faith in ourselves and one another."

TALKING, LISTENING, WRITING

6. Encourage candid personal testimony here. You may want to suggest this question as the topic for a journal entry.

7. Note that newspaper editors delight in the unsung hero motif.

8. Do your students recognize role models other than athletes or celebrities?

PROJECTS

9. You might want to ask students to focus on a test area, such as the peace process in the Near East or Greenpeace initiatives currently in the news.

THINKING ABOUT CONNECTIONS

There is a good opportunity here to counteract negativism.

Robert Bly, "The Community of Men"   435

Concepts of manhood or manliness have in recent years come in for much re-examination. Bly says, "By the time a man is thirty-five he knows that the images of the right man, the tough man, the true man which he received in high school do not work in life." Because such a man "is open to new visions of what a man is or could be," Bly sets out to provide leadership and inspiration.

THE RESPONSIVE READER

1. Bly's fourth paragraph addresses man's dark side. He traces this "dark side" to cultural, environmental, and biological factors (genetic inheritance). Part of the cultural cause is defined as "defective mythologies." These myths "ignore masculine depth of feeling, assign men a place in the sky instead of earth, teach obedience to the wrong powers, work to keep men boys, and entangle both men and women in systems of industrial domination that exclude both matriarchy and patriarchy." Man's "dark side" has led to "mad exploitation of earth resources, devaluation and humiliation of women, and obsession with tribal warfare."

2. As Bly describes four models from the nation's early history, each model is geographically defined. In New England, there was the "old-man-minded farmer" of the 1630s, who was "proud of his introversion" and was "willing to sit through three services in an unheated church." "An expansive, motherbound cavalier developed" in the South. The "greedy railroad entrepreneur" arose to industrialize the Northeast. In the West the culture was characterized by a "reckless I-will-do-without culture." A "cavalier" is an aristocrat trained in horsemanship and weaponry and presumably gallant manners. "Saturnian," (after the Roman god) is here used in the sense of the more common saturnine, connoting someone who is of a cold and steady mood, who acts only after grave deliberation, and who has a gloomy air.

3. The workaholic, disciplined fifties male "got to work early, labored responsibly, supported his wife and children, and admired discipline." He "was supposed to like football, be aggressive, stick up for the United States, never cry, and always provide." Although the fifties male "had a clear vision of what a man was, and what male responsibilities were," his underlying isolation made that "clear vision" "dangerous." The strengths of the fifties male include discipline, consistency, and the acceptance of responsibility for himself and his family. His view of the "culture and America's part in it was boyish and optimistic," and a number of his basic qualities "were strong and positive." "Underneath the charm and bluff" of the fifties male, however, there existed "much isolation, deprivation, and passivity." In fact, unless the fifties male "has an enemy, he isn't sure that he is alive." "Receptive space or intimate space was missing in this image of a man," and the personality "lacked some sense of flow," while the "psyche lacked compassion."

4. The key quality of the soft, sensitive sixties male was the development of his feminine consciousness. Unlike the fifties male, sixties males questioned "whether they knew what an adult male really was" and refused to take mindless patriotism to the extent of beating the drum in support of the war in Vietnam. The rise of feminism in the sixties caused another divergence between the fifties and sixties male: "Meanwhile, the feminist movement encouraged men to actually look at women, forcing them to become conscious of concerns and sufferings that the Fifties male labored

to avoid." The sixties male is "more thoughtful, more gentle," and the development of the feminine side is a process Bly finds "wonderful" and "important." On the other hand, Bly worries that this process has not made men "more free." Indeed, "He's a nice boy who pleases not only his mother but also the young woman he is living with." Bly misses some of the firm and unquestioning backbone that fifties men were allowed to pretend they had.

5. Bly's ideal male will have undergone the process to develop his feminine side, but he will also have acquired other attributes during the process. He will be capable of the necessary fierceness every relationship needs "once in a while." He will have "resolve." He will be able to articulate what he wants and to stand by his declaration. "The journey many American men have taken into softness, or receptivity," Bly concludes, "has been an immensely valuable journey, but more travel lies ahead." The mythical and literary precedents upon which Bly draws include Greek myths, the Arthurian legends, and Homer's story of Odysseus' arduous trip back to Ithaca from Troy.

TALKING, LISTENING, WRITING

6. Can the conservative revolution of the nineties be seen as a comeback of the fifties male? Is today's proverbial "angry white male" a throwback to the fifties image?

7. When Bly says that the system of "industrial domination" excludes "both matriarchy and patriarchy," he seems to have in mind a kind of idealized pre-industrial patriarchal tradition where men were not yet reduced to cowed and exploited cogs in the machine. While Bly speaks admiringly of strong, assertive women, he is calling on men to be more assertive in turn. According to Bly, "soft" men who are "not happy" and lack energy, are often seen "with strong women who positively radiate energy." This is because "The strong or life-giving woman who graduated from the sixties . . . played an important part in producing this life-preserving, but not life-giving, man." Bly's mythological precedents nostalgically evoke a roaming, adventurous, dominant male who may seem anachronistic to many readers. (You might want to let students have fun scripting and performing skits titled "Ulysses in the Dorm" or "Odysseus in the Faculty Lounge" or the like.)

8. A study of the media treatment of any of the last four or five presidents (with the possible exception of President Reagan) might help students understand debunking as a time-honored American tradition, comparable to the ritual sacrifice of the god-king in early cultures.

9. Does *ideal* here have to mean utopian or impossibly romanticized?

PROJECTS

10. Encourage students to draw up these portraits in terms of both real-life examples (Maya Lin, architect; Sally Ride, astronaut; Jackie Joyner-

Kersee, athlete; and Janet Reno, attorney general) and literary or mythological precedents.

Shann Nix, "O. J. Mania: American Tragedy"   440

The O. J. Simpson case may qualify as the most overreported, overanalyzed, and overexploited legal trial of the twentieth century. Shann Nix uses the case as a starting point in this essay on heroes and their inevitable destruction. Once our heroes have failed to live up to our over-optimistic expectations, we eagerly change course from adulation to condemnation.

THE RESPONSIVE READER

1. In traditional myth and story, the hero comes to a tragic end, according to Michael Nagler, professor emeritus of classics and comparative literature at the University of California, Berkeley. Nagler says: "There is only one ending to the story of the hero"—a tragic one: "They get it in the teeth every time." From traditional myth and story, Nix uses the example of Joan of Arc. Her other examples are more contemporary: John Fitzgerald Kennedy, Malcolm X, Martin Luther King, Jr., Abraham Lincoln. Possible additional examples from literature: from Sophocles, Oedipus, and Antigone; from Euripides, Iphigenia, and Andromache; from Aeschylus, Prometheus; from Plutarch, Brutus, Mark Antony, and Julius Caesar; and from Shakespeare, Lear, Hamlet, and Othello.

2. Some of the trappings of celebrity in our society are expensive cars ("the Rolls Royce, the Bentley, the Ferrari"), extravagant toys ("the pool, the Jacuzzi, the tennis court, the basketball court, the playground"), and ostentatious homes ("The house that cost $5 million. The $2 million summer house at Laguna Beach. The New York apartment"). There are "the adulation, the movie roles, the wild parties." A "beautiful blonde wife" seems de rigueur for the fawned-over celebrity male. Our juvenile pampering of celebrities includes fawning favoritism at restaurants, illegally parked cars that go unticketed, special dispensations from virtually everyone, and constant press exposure.

3. When Nix lists "George Bush, Ronald Reagan, Jimmy Carter, Gerald Ford, Richard Nixon," it is a continuous and bipartisan list of presidents who have, to varying degrees, been vilified once we have discovered "that he's a human being, like the rest of us." She says, "We build up a Bill Clinton as the savior who will solve all of our problems and then we tear him down" once we realize he is not Hercules and the Augean stables will remain uncleansed. Nix does a fairly convincing job of showing the reader that the "hatchet job" we do on our politicians is similar to the job we do on celebrities?

4. Nix quotes Rene Girard's theory that the scapegoat absorbs, albeit temporarily, the violent impulses of a society. Girard calls this the "fairly

unpleasant way" humans have developed "to deal with violence." "We scoop up all that nasty anger and dump it onto one person. Then we destroy that person, and feel better—for a while." Thus, during a time of war, drought, famine, or disease, a scapegoat would be sacrificed: "orphans, or the mentally disturbed, or the physically handicapped. Or animals. Captive soldiers from another tribe." Christ may be viewed as a scapegoat who claimed to have taken the sins of mankind upon himself and was sacrificed by the Romans. Dionysus, in *The Bacchae,* is sacrificed as a scapegoat for the violence of his frenzied followers. In "times of great social stress," a goat or an orphan or a slave will not suffice; the king himself must die. Thus, we observe the best and brightest with a disturbing mixture of feelings: admiration is mixed with pity, jealousy is counterbalanced by terror, and love is diminished by loathing.

The link between the warriors of old and football heroes of today is that the former of necessity have been replaced by the latter. "So O. J.," Nix says, "or any professional football player—is a sort of stand-in warrior." Since most of us will not personally be doing any fighting, we use football players (or soccer players or boxers or hockey players) as proxies, and through them we give vent to our own violent tendencies. One of the reasons that most of us will not be doing any fighting is that far too many of us are couch potatoes. We are sedentary and overweight and quite happy to let "football players play out our violent fantasies for us."

5. The problem with scapegoats, Nix says, is that they only relieve "the tensions in a society briefly." A scapegoat is not a permanent solution to the violence and stress of a society: "pretty soon we're looking around for someone else to sacrifice." The moral of the Simpson tale is that if we "weren't trapped in the cycle" of targeting scapegoats as "the root of all our problems," and then destroying them, we would not be shocked when our heroes behave in exactly the manner we've taught them (i.e., violently—and the number of maimed and killed innocents might be reduced. The point of the Simpson story should not be that he is a fallen hero who will be destroyed because he has not lived up to our expectations. It should be that a large number of people are suffering (the two victims, "the kids and the families"), and we have appropriated this suffering "as entertainment." What society should learn from this story is that we should play "football ourselves instead of hiring people to do it for us"; that we should use "all the money we spend on professional football to stop crime"; that we should stop glamorizing violence; that we should not be hypocrites when our heroes behave exactly as they've been trained; and that we should look for heroes who are "gentle people," who work to stop violence, "instead of mercenary warriors."

6. One glimpse of the violent side of Simpson's nature is the picture of his wife "running out of the house to greet police wearing a bra and sweat pants, nursing a cut lip and a black eye, screaming 'He's going to kill me.'" As for the other side of the coin, Simpson was born in "the projects" and suffered from rickets (a childhood condition of soft, deformed bones caused by insufficient Vitamin D). "His parents correct this with a homemade brace, forcing each foot into the wrong shoe," suggesting that Simpson's parents were impoverished and unable to pay for medical attention for their

son. Simpson worked hard to "escape the streets by improving his grades and learning to play football." As a result, he is accepted at the University of Southern California "where he majors in sociology and wins the Heisman Trophy." He goes on to great success as a professional football player and "upon retirement gains admission into the new old-boy network of corporate America and plays a few roles in silly movies."

TALKING, LISTENING, WRITING

7. When Nix observes that a person trained to violence often has a hard time reining in such behaviors, she is not so much excusing Simpson as condemning the rest of us for acting surprised when such things happen. Nix is not concerned so much with Simpson's guilt or innocence as with ours.

8. Such matters as the failure of the justice system to protect Nicole Simpson, or the tactics of high-priced lawyers, or the possible limitations of the jury system do not become major issues here.

9. Classic examples of scapegoating include anti-semitism in post–World War I Germany and anti-foreigner or anti-immigrant agitation in this country in times of an economic downward spiral.

Alice Walker, "In Search of Our Mothers' Gardens"   447

"Whatever rocky soil" Alice Walker's mother landed on, "she turned into a garden." In this essay, Walker explores the never completely stifled creativity of anonymous African American women of earlier generations. Walker draws on a rich fund of family memories, her reading of both canonized and minority authors, remembered recordings and performances of black singers, and her visits to institutions like the Smithsonian.

THE RESPONSIVE READER

1. Walker's central lesson is that the creative spirit can never be completely crushed. Even in the face of overwhelming obstacles, African American women created beauty and symmetry in their bleak world. Although traditional creative outlets were closed to these women, they created art in quilts and gardens that were testimony of their capacity for beauty and emotion.

2. Among outstanding black artists and writers whose memory Walker invokes, the poet Phillis Wheatley, the novelist Zora Neale Hurston, and the singers Bessie Smith, Ma Rainey, and Roberta Flack are likely to be most familiar. Walker uses Jean Toomer as a point of departure for her essay. Toomer recorded his perceptions of the unrealized creative gifts of the women whom Walker claims as "our mothers and grandmothers," and he recognized the need of "a larger life for their expression." The British

novelist Virginia Woolf also wrote about women whose gifts were stifled—"a lost novelist, a suppressed poet . . . some mute and inglorious Jane Austen." Walker reminds us that African American women faced the obstacles not merely of repressive convention but of "chains, guns, the lash, the ownership of one's body by someone else, submission to an alien religion."

3. Walker refuses to view Phillis Wheatley as a "fool" for celebrating a golden-haired goddess of liberty in the poetic style of her eighteenth-century white masters. Walker sees Wheatley as an artist who had the urge to create—in whatever mode or medium available to her. The particulars of Wheatley's life—captured in Africa at seven and made the slave of whites who instilled in her the notion they had rescued her from barbarism—meant that "her loyalties were completely divided, as was, without question, her mind." Therefore, Walker concludes, what Wheatley sang was not important. What mattered was that Wheatley "kept alive, in so many of our ancestors, the notion of song."

4. Walker's mother becomes a role model as a hugely overworked woman who managed to find an outlet for her creative spirit. The daughter celebrates her as "radiant, almost to the point of being invisible—except as Creator, hand and eye. . . . Ordering the universe in the image of her personal conception of beauty." The mother "planted ambitious gardens" and worked on them after or before an exhausting day. "Even my memories of poverty are seen through a screen of blooms."

TALKING, LISTENING, WRITING

5. and 7.–8. Bad parenting and memories of martinet teachers play major roles in our current societal lore. In talking or writing about people they do admire, students should be encouraged to stay clear of clichéd or dutiful praise.

6. Future art and music majors might take the lead in this discussion?

PROJECTS

9. How much of the lore about national leaders, revolutionary heroes, outstanding athletes, or inspirational artists is passed on to a younger generation?

Martin Luther King, Jr., "I Have a Dream"   457

In this famous speech, Martin Luther King, Jr., speaks passionately about his hope for the emergence of a new just and truly equal American society. He reassures the white majority by his commitment to the philosophy of nonviolence while at the same time appealing eloquently to the promise of human dignity and equal rights that gives meaning to American history.

THE RESPONSIVE READER

1. The great political confrontations are fought in part by means of weighty words, loaded words, and fighting words. *Emancipation* means emerging from the bonds of servitude and of debilitating ignorance and alludes to Lincoln's Emancipation Proclamation by which the slaves were set free; for King, the proclamation "came as a joyous daybreak to end the long night of captivity." *Segregation* was a legally sanctioned all-pervasive social system that forced African Americans to go to separate schools, to live in separate neighborhoods, to use separate restrooms, to ride in the back of buses. ("We don't serve Negroes here.") The fight against legalized segregation was at the center of the civil rights movement. *Gradualism* was a policy of accommodation that promised slow changes for the better to people willing to wait—a mentality that King vehemently rejects in favor of "now." *Brotherhood* has both religious and political connotations (it was one of the slogans of the French Revolution). King uses the word to emphasize the brotherhood of all human beings regardless of race. *Militancy* means aggressive and at times violent action in support of a cause; King uses the word without the connotation of violence. *Civil rights* include freedom of speech and assembly, the right to due process, the right to vote, and equality before the law. Civil rights became the rallying cry of the movement to assure equality before the law and economic opportunity for minorities. *Police brutality* became a watchword of civil rights groups protesting the routine harassment and abuse of minorities—beatings, false arrests, "excessive use of force"—by predominantly white police. *The American Dream* is the idea that all human beings deserve an equal chance and have the right to their place in the sun; for multitudes, America held out the promise of a new society without the exploitation of labor, the gross inequalities of wealth, and the encrusted privilege of the Old World. *Interposition* is the concept that a state (in King's speech, Alabama) may reject a federal mandate (school integration) by claiming the Federal Government is infringing upon the state's rights. *Nullification* is implementation of interposition, as when a state refuses to implement a Federal law.

2. King's strength was his powerful appeal to shared values. He aimed at making the white majority see racial segregation as a legacy of slavery by attacking the "manacles of segregation and the chains of discrimination." His basic strategy was to take whites by their word as they mouthed the "magnificent words" of their constitutional documents. He mobilized for his cause some of the most basic commitments of Americans: the belief in liberty ("Let freedom ring"), the belief that all "are created equal," and the religious injunction to think of your fellow human being as your brother.

3. King's basic plea to blacks was that moral suasion would prove more powerful than the politics of riot and violent revolution. At the same time King spoke most directly to "my people," he also warned them: "In the process of gaining our rightful place we must not be guilty of wrongful deeds." He warned against the use of "physical violence," and asserted the struggle must occur "on the high plane of dignity and discipline," without resorting "to a distrust of all white people."

4. King's basic assumption about the white majority was that "their destiny is tied up with our destiny and their freedom is inextricably bound to our freedom." He appealed to a basic sense of fairness and justice by dramatizing the plight of the disadvantaged living "on a lonely island of poverty in the midst of a vast ocean of material prosperity."

TALKING, LISTENING, WRITING

5. The politics of violent confrontation, the exploitation of incendiary incidents, and the eruption of riots resulting in large-scale loss of life and property may seem to have largely superseded the politics of nonviolent protest.

6. Cynicism about tweedledee-tweedledum political choices is widespread. Yet such events as the 1992 election of several female Senators to what was long essentially a male club do at times remind people of the power of the vote?

7. Note that these are very volatile questions.

PROJECTS

8. The Reverend Jesse Jackson, Illinois' Carol Moseley-Braun, Virginia's Douglas Wilder, California's Willie Brown, and ex-mayor David Dinkins of New York are examples of leaders who have received extensive press coverage. Controversial figures like Justice Clarence Thomas or the Reverend Al Sharpton have received extensive media scrutiny.

THINKING ABOUT CONNECTIONS

Though couched in different language, both selections are anchored in a generous faith in the capacity of people to overcome divisions and antagonism. King addresses the need for a change of heart on a national scale, while Milk thinks in terms of regenerating a city neighborhood by neighborhood.

Short Story

Tillie Olsen, "I Stand Here Ironing"   462

Olsen became a hero and role model to many in the women's movement for her defiance of the odds that keep working-class women silent and for the powerful uncompromising candor and honesty of her writing. In this widely reprinted story, as the narrator stands and does her ironing, a request from her daughter's teacher sends the woman back in time. The teacher wants the mother to come in and talk about the daughter, but, as the mother remembers the particulars of the daughter's life, it is clear that her child of "depression, of war, of fear" is not going to be reached as a result of a chat with her teacher.

THE RESPONSIVE READER

1. This is a story of catharsis, of trying to come to terms with a troubling, traumatic past? The narrator is trying to exorcise a sense of guilt about something of which she as Emily's mother is not guilty—the workings of a situation that despite exhausting efforts is beyond the mother's control, the logic of poverty-stricken and stunted lives. Olsen wrote the story to explain how circumstances—the husband's abandonment of the family, poverty, repressive schools, convalescent homes—combine to influence the life of a child far more than the child's mother could have done. "There is all that life that has happened outside of me, beyond me," the mother says. The "you" in the story is specifically the daughter's teacher (but more generally it is also the reader)? The story illuminates a bleak and tragic time and is the writer's explanation of as well as her resignation to what has happened: "I will never total it all," she says.

2. The woman's outlook is that of a person who accepts what must be done in order to assure her survival and that of her children. Although her eight-month-old daughter "was a miracle" to the mother, she was forced to leave the child during the day "with the woman downstairs to whom she was no miracle at all." The mother is aware of the compromises she made and knows whatever happens in the future is heavily influenced by the daughter's reaction to the compromises—the stays with relatives, the "evil" teacher at day care, the convalescent home. Whatever the mother's feelings about the daughter's misery, "it would have made no difference." Poverty forced the woman into inevitable decisions. It also taught the woman not to have expectations, especially for her daughter: "So all that is in her will not bloom—but in how many does it? There is still enough left to live by."

3. The narrator finds herself in a callous, threatening, and hostile outside world. Both the institutions and the individuals are threats to the mother's and daughter's happy and satisfying life together. The institutions are places bereft of love, full of inane rules, run by "overworked and exasperated teachers," administrators, and caretakers. When the power of the institutions combines with the meanness of the individuals—a father who abandons his family to poverty, the teacher who taunts a frightened child— the result is a child who walks timidly and without joy. An occasional kind individual offers help or advice: The old man "in his gentle way" tried to get the mother to show her love for Emily instead of the anxious face she typically showed; it was a lesson that benefited the other children, but it came "too late for Emily."

4. As a child, Emily must have felt abandoned and left in the care of people who treated her badly. She must have felt resentment at a younger sibling apparently more privileged and loved than she was herself. At nineteen Emily cannot believe far enough into the future to justify taking mid-term examinations. Since Emily has never known sustained comfort and

security it is not surprising she thinks that quite soon "we'll all be atom-dead" and nothing will matter at all. A gift for mimicry becomes a redeeming feature in the daughter's downbeat, circumscribed temperament: "Out of her despair," Emily would imitate "happenings or types at school," and the mother learns Emily has "a gift for comedy."

5. "My wisdom came too late" for the child's benefit the mother tells the reader, and she concedes her love was anxious rather than proud. There is nothing the mother can do now, and, with identical circumstances, very little she could have done differently then. Therefore she wants Emily to live the way that Emily wishes, but with the knowledge that she is not "helpless before the iron," as her mother was.

TALKING, LISTENING, WRITING

6. Part of the strength of Olsen's story is her painstaking accounting for decisions made under the pressure of unrelenting circumstances. Make sure criticism or defense takes into account the givens of the mother's situation?

7. Social workers and teachers tend to see situations from their own self-justifying point of view that may be very different from that of a parent?

8. Younger students, sympathizing with Emily, may have a headstart in experimenting with this change in point of view.

PROJECTS

9. For starters: According to the census bureau, the number of people defined as poor (family of four earning less than $13,924 or individuals earning less than $6,932) in 1991 comprised 14.2 percent of the population, for a total of 35.7 million, the highest number since 1964.

THINKING ABOUT CONNECTIONS

Parker seems to focus on poor Americans largely ignored or written off by society, whereas Olsen is often contending with institutions that offer more hindrance than help?

Poem

Pamela Alexander, "Flight (for Amelia Earhart)"   470

In this poem, Alexander evokes Amelia Earhart's doomed attempt to fly around the world. On June 2, 1937, Earhart's plane vanished near Howland Island in the South Pacific. No one knows how or where Earhart died, although William Manchester in *The Glory and the Dream* asserts that Earhart had spotted Japanese fortifications on the Marianas and was subsequently "almost certainly forced down and murdered" by the Japanese. Alexander says, "The last square has / an island in it, but does not / show her where." "The last square" is located at the approximate point where the international date line and the equator meet, in the vast expanse of the Pacific Ocean.

THE RESPONSIVE READER

1. The paradoxical "organized adventure"—seemingly an oxymoron or self-canceling phrase—upon reflection makes practical sense. An odyssey like Earhart's could not have happened without massive organization and planning. Ulysses is the Roman name for the Greek hero Odysseus, the central figure of Homer's *The Odyssey* as well as one of the major figures in *The Iliad*. Like Ulysses, Earhart is on an odyssey (a long wandering or journey characterized by unpredictable changes in fortune). The adjectives most often used by Homer to describe Ulysses are cunning and wily, and Alexander echoes this description with the statement, "Carelessness / offends the spirit of Ulysses." Again, Alexander pays homage to Homer by using Homer's words to describe Earhart's adventure: "Flight / above the wine-dark shining flood / is order." Thus, Ulysses' role in this poem is as the prototypical adventurer, in whose shoes Earhart hopes (in Tennyson's words) "To strive, to seek, to find, and not to yield."

2. The sights, sounds, and sensations of the journey include "the fragrance of blooming / orange orchards" carried up to the pilot's nostrils; the shadows of trees upon the land ("No one has seen a tree / who has not seen it from the air, with / its shadow"); and geographical phenomena like the sluggish and brown Amazon River, the cranes and storks around "huge, shallow" Lake Chad, the blueness of the Red Sea, and the greenness of the White and Blue Nile Rivers. Alexander's images of stars on strings and the plane as a "tiny gear that turns the world" are both seen from inside the cockpit of the Electra. From the cramped pilot's chair the plane is seen as a gear upon which the world turns. The perspective has changed so that the stars are shaken "down their strings until / they hang outside the cockpit, close enough / to touch"—Earhart has not traveled up to meet the heavens; the heavens instead have come down to meet the plane.

3. The journey has been divided into white squares upon a map, "each / an hour's flying time." When all the squares have been flown over, the journey will be finished. Despite the organized nature of this adventure, some things elude planning. Out in the remote South Pacific in 1937, Earhart tried to find an island to correspond with the island depicted in her "last square." At the end of the poem, the plane slowly runs out of fuel, like the sand slowly running out in an hourglass, often symbolizing the running out of time and the approach of death. The squares introduce the journey and they also end it, since they appear both at the beginning and the end of the poem. Life can be measured similarly, as a series of white squares that must be crossed before journey's end.

TALKING, LISTENING, WRITING

4. As compared to Earhart's time, there are more inspirational female sports and adventure figures today. Your class may want to organize a tribute to some of the women mentioned and others.

5. An example of the traditional reluctance to credit women's achievement might be the case of Lt. Kara Hultgreen, the first female combat squadron pilot to die while flying for the Navy. In October of 1994, the F14A Tomcat she was flying went into a stall as she approached an aircraft carrier off the California coast. After her death, it was asserted that the only reason she was flying an F14A was preferential treatment because of her sex and that because she was a woman she was not able to pilot an F14A as well as a man. However, the Navy brass concluded an investigation into Hultgreen's death by determining that engine failure, not pilot error, had been responsible for the crash.

PROJECTS

6. Elizabeth Blackwell (1821–1910) was the first woman in the United States to receive a medical degree. Marie Curie (1867–1934) shared the 1903 Nobel Prize in physics and became the first person to win a second Nobel Prize, which she did in 1911, in chemistry, for her discovery of polonium and radium. Margaret Mead (1901–1978) was an anthropologist who studied the peoples of Oceana and authored widely read books such as *Coming of Age in Samoa.*

CHAPTER 9

LANGUAGE: Bond or Barrier

Linguists have invested tremendous intellectual effort into analyzing the complex technical workings of language that are largely beyond the reach of traditional school grammar. At the same time, semanticists and sociolinguists have studied the role language plays in human interaction. Much of this work has been cautionary, warning against abuses of language: loaded words prejudging issues, words that demean and belittle, words that incite or inflame. In recent years, linguists and educators have increasingly explored the implications of the fact that millions of Americans are bilingual. Should society help immigrants and the children of immigrants maintain their original language? Or should the educational system push full speed toward making people fully proficient in English as the national language? What should our attitude be toward students coming to school speaking a social or regional dialect ("black English")?

Deborah Tannen, "Talk in the Intimate Relationship: His and Hers"

Like other students of interpersonal communication, Tannen's basic assumption is that men and women have different ways of talking. In the very first sentence of "Talk in the Intimate Relationship," Tannen calls the difference between the way men and women converse "cross-cultural." With culturally conditioned differences between what men and women say and also between what men and women hear (or read between the lines), it is not surprising that men and women often fail to communicate.

THE RESPONSIVE READER

1. According to Tannen, women are more attuned to the metamessages— the overtones and implications of what is said—than the men to whom they are talking. Quite apart from what is literally said, what people say shows how they feel about one another. Women, who value "involvement" more than men, are quicker to pick up on such vibrations? Women are more "sensitized"; they have better antennae. By the same token, they expect their partners to sense what is expected without the woman having to spell it out in so many words?

2. Some examples: Being preoccupied with interpersonal relations, women may tend to think a frown means they did something wrong when the man is really pondering what to eat. Tannen's example of the fiftieth anniversary cake illustrates how men focus on the message and women focus on the metamessage. Men already stuffed at an anniversary dinner have no problem with putting off the cake until the next day's lunch, while for the women what matters is the thought, the ritual, the symbolic value of sharing

the cake? Pronouns are a special problem: A man may say, "I am going for a walk." He means, "I'm going for a walk—and you can come if you want to." But the woman is likely to hear, "I'm going for a walk—without you."

3.   Once a misunderstanding has occurred, it is exacerbated when each partner starts arguing the logic and rationality of his or her own position?

4.   Tannen's most prominent male stereotype—the strong silent type—is quite familiar and is constantly reinforced by television and Hollywood. Westerns and war stories for decades presented cryptic brooding men who did not waste words? (Films with Sylvester Stallone or Clint Eastwood tend to be full of brooding silences?)

5.   Tannen's hope for miscommunicating couples lies in a different approach: Women might try to believe "what he says" and not what they sense. Each partner can modify his or her "ways of talking" while accepting the ways of the other partner. Men could learn to listen and to talk more?

TALKING, LISTENING, WRITING

6.   For the purposes of her argument, Tannen makes sweeping generalizations? Men do not all interpret words strictly literally, and some do listen to and empathize with women's problems? Women do not always take offense at the man's use of the singular pronoun, and some do enjoy "paying attention to scientific explanations and facts?" Many men are quick to read between the lines and are quick to bristle at imagined slights and implications?

7.   People often find themselves using the lingo of a peer group. They may feel the pressure to be witty or arrogant or blasé when their own personal inclinations tend in a different reaction.

PROJECTS

8.   The language of the sports pages, like that of the society pages has its own clichés, kinds of hyperbole, euphemisms, allusions, invocation of idols, etc?

Amoja Three Rivers, "Cultural Etiquette: A Guide"   492

For Amoja Three Rivers, "all people are people." The very act of labeling people as a minority, as Jewish, or as black already implies "different from us, not one of us." This article probes the many subtle and overt ways in which language serves "racial and cultural discrimination."

THE RESPONSIVE READER

1. Stereotypes such as the passionate Latin lover, the forever inscrutably smiling and bowing Japanese, or the stoic taciturn Indian may to some extent have been removed from current commercials, but they flourish in many sources like reruns and old movies? For this author, all the familiar clichés about ethnic or cultural groups, from the flashing eyes of Latin women to the wealth of Jews are odious because they make people seem different and put them outside the group to which we owe loyalty.

2. The author objects to many familiar labels that make whole groups of people sound different, inferior, weird, or unreliable. Three Rivers objects to *minority* because it is "statistically incorrect" (on a global scale, affluent whites are a small minority), "ethnocentric," and reinforces the otherness of a group; she objects to *exotic* because it is "ethnocentric and racist" when used to describe people; and she objects to *cult* because the term is perceived as pejorative and is not (although it could be) used to refer to all religions. *Half-breed* is objectionable because the "inference that a person's 'race' depends on blood is racist"; reverse racism, unlike real racism, does not cause segregation, exclusion, or exploitation. Three Rivers objects to the key term *race* because 500,000 years of genetic crisscrossing have made the term "meaningless."

3. Three Rivers warns against familiar ploys and rationalizations: confessing "past racist transgressions"; describing another's racial prejudices; assuming that people are "wrong or paranoid or oversensitive" if they speaks out "about their own oppression." The author is allergic to whites who brag about "overseas trips to our homeland" or showing off the "expensive artifacts" brought back from such trips.

4. *Ethnocentric* describes an absorption in the traditions and supposed superiority of one's own ethnic group; the charge of ethnocentricity is at the bottom of many of the author's criticisms of white society. *Anti-Semitism* is hostility toward and discrimination against Jews: to the author, it is one outstanding, age-old manifestation of the racist impulse. *Bigotry* is an intolerant, prejudicial, and obstinate devotion to one's own church, party, belief, or opinion. *Genocide* is the deliberate and systematic destruction of an entire national or ethnic group. It was first used to describe Nazi Germany's methodical extermination of the Jews.

5. She may at times seem oversensitive, but many of her warnings against the invidious use of language make good sense on second thought—including her advice not to use terms such as *gestapo* or *concentration camp* loosely?

TALKING, LISTENING, WRITING

6. The author makes a good case that our language—if not our thinking or basic commitments—is shot through with crassly and subtly outgrouping pejorative words of all kinds?

7. Members of the comfortable white majority may tend to bristle at many of the author's strictures.

8. Our language seems to have a vast repertory of words that put people down or box them in, with the putdowns young people encounter in school— *fatso, retard, dumbo, nerd, geek, faggot, slut*—only the tip of the iceberg?

PROJECTS

9. Students may be able to find accounts of relevant initiatives and discussions in student newspapers as well as the local press.

Carol Padden and Tom Humphries, "Deaf in America: A Changing Consciousness"   497

The way we treat people with physical disabilities has changed greatly in the last few decades, and so especially also has the way we talk and think about them. The author of this article would prefer for us to think of deaf people not as disabled but as people with a rich culture of their own.

THE RESPONSIVE READER

1. The authors' aim is to make us see sign language (actually several rival signing systems) not as "impoverished" but as human language "with a potential for rich expression." Sign language, like language generally, is made up of small elements that together create meaning. (Morphemes—such as the semantic unit *tree* and the plural *s*—are the smallest meaningful units in spoken language, as certain handshapes are in sign language). Sign language, like spoken language, serves to explain, to brag, to express patriotism, to give vent to playfulness, to entertain.

2. Readers who think of deaf people as isolated may be surprised by the sense of solidarity and the community activities chronicled in this article.

3. Poetry often seems to stretch the limits of normal language, both in its spoken and signed forms.

4. Even communicating a fairly simple "statement" would be an achievement?

TALKING, LISTENING, WRITING

5. People with disabilities and their families have in recent years become much less reticent about sharing their experiences and exploring the challenges.

6. Access to businesses, public buildings, and public transportation has been a major issue in recent years.

7. A videotape of a program with an interpreter for the hearing-impaired may have to do.

Jorge R. Mancillas: "Bilingualism: Assimilation Is More Than ABCs" 512

The tug-of-war over bilingual education has for years been a major focus of the struggle between the conservative and the liberal forces trying to shape the future of American education. Representing one pole of this argument, Mancillas argues that English must be taught in tandem with schooling in a child's native language.

THE RESPONSIVE READER

1. Mancillas effectively dramatizes the struggle faced by even a well-prepared second-language student. Few monolingual Americans understand that the C or B a second-language student achieves at Berkeley may represent a Herculean effort well beyond that invested by other students to get an A. The challenge is not only a new language—an incredibly complex and subtle instrument—but also an easy familiarity with the myriad ramifications of national history, high culture, and popular culture. Mancillas believes that without instruction in their own language bilingual students in the public schools, without the background and support he had, are bound to be way behind academically and traumatized by failure by the time they achieve full proficiency in English.

2. English-only, sink-or-swim policies will merely aggravate the already horrendous dropout and failure rates and help swell the ranks of an alienated, unemployable, violence-prone underclass.

3. Mancillas opts for the maintenance model of bilingual education, with second-language students "preserving their original language and cultural skills." This way these students could make a valuable contribution to the education of other students, drawing on their "birthright familiarity with Latin American, Asian, or Middle Eastern societies." They would be the "bridge-builders this country needs to succeed in the global community."

TALKING, LISTENING, WRITING

4. You may want to organize a panel giving bilingual students the opportunity to share their own experiences.

5. The drive toward "culturally insular" and ethnically "clean" nation states has been a major destructive political force throughout the twentieth century. Mancillas invokes the traditional liberal ideal of a "pluralistic" America, which may have been slowly superseded by the often-voiced

commitment to "diversity" (now increasingly under attack). As with the "global" perspective, Mancillas here very briefly invokes ideals that are in danger of becoming yesterday's slogans?

PROJECTS

6. Much vocal criticism has characterized the backlash against bilingual education. Much has been made, for instance, of the "tower-of-Babel" effect of printing ballot propositions in half a dozen or more languages and of the difficulty of finding teachers qualified to teach in Samoan, Tagalog, Mandarin, Laotian, and Vietnamese.

Richard Rodriguez, "Aria: A Memoir of a Bilingual Childhood"   516

Richard Rodriguez' *Hunger of Memory* has been widely read as a candid record of the painful transition and change of identity that children of immigrants experience as they leave the language (and culture) of their parents behind. Rodriguez was attacked by other Mexican Americans for his apparent willingness to leave his Mexican background behind as the price for of a new "public identity." By the same token, he seemed to confirm the doubts of skeptics about the possibilities of true bilingual and bicultural literacy.

THE RESPONSIVE READER

1. Rodriguez describes his first language as "a private language, my family's language." This was the language of intimacy that he gradually had to leave behind as he adopted English, the public language of the larger society. When he heard the sounds of Spanish, the boy understood that they were "the pleasing, soothing, consoling reminder that one was at home." The limitation of language so defined is that it is confined to inside the home. Until his teachers visited his home, Rodriguez' mother and father spoke to him exclusively in Spanish. They used English hesitatingly or haltingly when talking to a stranger or in public, hampered in their dealings with "los gringos."

2. Young Richard's public schooling proceeded on the traditional model of assimilation and acculturation. Hearing his name spoken in English was Rodriguez' initiation into his second language. During that school year, his teachers insisted Rodriguez speak "public English," they visited his home to request that his parents encourage the children "to practice their English at home," and they required "daily tutoring sessions." This led up to the day when the boy raised his hand and volunteered a confident response in English to a teacher's question. When Rodriguez' parents had to speak English, the boy listened "uneasily," aware that his "clutching trust in their protection and power" had been weakened. Once the parents spoke only in English to

their children, Rodriguez' family life was "greatly changed." The mother's "became the public voice," communication between parent and child in English lost its spontaneity, and the father became far more retiring and seemingly inarticulate.

3. Rodriguez' success in school came about at the expense of the intimate relationship he had with his parents. English created a growing gulf. "I no longer knew what words to use in addressing my parents." "Once I learned the public language, it would never again be easy for me to hear intimate family voices." However, he is quick to assert that this "loss implies the gain," and that, despite the price, he knows it was only when he began to think of himself as an American that he could "seek the rights and opportunities necessary for full public individuality."

4. Rodriguez describes the day he spoke up in class as the day his "childhood started to end." He finally finds himself at a point where Spanish-speaking people sound strange to him and he to them?

TALKING, LISTENING, WRITING

5. People under intense public scrutiny sometimes develop a public persona very different from their private personalities?

6. As Rodriguez' essay documents, this opting for one identity or another or for a dual identity is an intensely personal experience. Today many of the most visible and successful Mexican Americans (in the media, in politics) seem to be accomplished bilinguals?

7. Students (and some faculty) have at times made heroic efforts to mask regional or down-home accents?

PROJECTS

8. Some sample questions: How do the police and the courts cope with language problems? How about the Department of Motor Vehicles, Social Security offices, and other agencies?

THINKING ABOUT CONNECTIONS

Rodriguez is Exhibit A for a full-immersion model (taking the child out of the first-language peer culture as well as home environment) that could not be replicated in schools and communities where the first-language culture is close to becoming the majority culture?

Jesse Birnbaum, "Substandard Bearer: A Dictionary of U.S. Slang"   527

Birnbaum says, "Slang may be substandard, the stepsister of Standard English, but it has enlivened the language for centuries." His use of slang in this article supports that assertion.

THE RESPONSIVE READER

1. One way to confirm that Birnbaum likes slang is to observe how much of it he manages to work into the article. From the beginning ("What kind of cockamamie lingo is slang anyway?") to the end ("The completed work promises to be one gollywhopper of a dictionary"), Birnbaum delights in the use of slang from A through G as he reviews the first of a planned three-volume dictionary on American slang. In addition, he points out that slang "is wonderfully expressive and endlessly inventive," and it has resisted purification since the days of Samuel Johnson. Indeed, there are numerous instances of slang actually forcing its way into the hallowed pages of the dictionaries, e.g., "blizzard, disk jockey and gadget."

2. As for the history of slang, English words were not divided into "good" and "bad" until the first dictionaries arrived, in the mid-seventeenth century. Before that, "Words and phrases that are today considered vulgar expressions for bodily and sexual functions were once common currency among men and women of all classes." As a result, "Everybody was vulgar, so nobody was vulgar." Once literacy became widespread, the development of slang and efforts to stop that development occurred simultaneously. Slang began to grow as a "private code" for the criminal classes and as "a subversive nose-thumbing at the Establishment" for people on the periphery. With such proliferation of new terms, the response of "writers and critics like Johnson" was to "formulate proscriptions" in an attempt to purify "the King's English." Such measures did not work in the seventeenth century and work only fitfully in the late twentieth century.

3. Slang tends to originate as the insider's language of "discrete groups for whom a special jargon affords status and protection," i.e., students, blacks, the military, the underworld, and drug and alcohol users. Another key feature of slang is its extensive coverage of off-color subjects: "scatology, illicit behavior, drunkenness, sex and genitalia." Much of the slang associated with the preceding is "unprintable." The endurance of some of the actual words and the subject matter is of interest: "Teenagers who grope (fondle) may be surprised to learn that lovers were groping in the 14th century." The use of "bad" for "good" dates back to 1897. "The most frequently used obscenity in the English tongue, the ever versatile F word," was used as early as the late fifteenth century. Twelve pages of the dictionary are devoted to the astonishing variety the word inspires.

TALKING, LISTENING, WRITING

4. You may want to arrange for a pooling of findings.

5. Are men more likely to swear or use vulgar language than women? Are blue-collar workers more likely to use it than office workers?

6. Students may want to investigate religious prohibitions on swearing (testifying to the fact that swearing goes back to the earliest known stages of culture)?

PROJECTS

7. In recent decades, dictionaries have been violently attacked (and banned) for their liberal stance. Are some more conservative than others?

Rachel L. Jones, "What's Wrong with Black English" 530

Rachel L. Jones presents her objections to "that colorful, grammar-to-the-winds patois that is black English" in this essay. She reminds her readers that African Americans successful and influential in this society—from Martin Luther King, Jr., to Andrew Young and Barbara Jordan—eloquently and effectively use standard English.

THE RESPONSIVE READER

1. Jones was made language-conscious first by the school bully who resented her talking "proper" and getting good grades. She again became vividly aware of her language problem when looking for an apartment. (She sounded white on the phone but looked black when she appeared at the door.) In school the lesson that came across was that "for many blacks, standard English is not only unfamiliar, it is socially unacceptable."

2. Jones' experience differs from that of many of her peers because she came from a family in which standard English was encouraged and practiced. The "importance of reading and learning" was continually emphasized. She read extensively from John Steinbeck and Ray Bradbury to the Bobbsey Twins. That does not mean that she cannot talk down-home English when at home.

3. Jones' "black peers" have confronted her with the question, "Why do you talk like you're white?" In addition, prominent African Americans like James Baldwin (who wrote beautiful eloquent literary English) have called black English a language that is vital, an effective political tool, and crucial to black identity. Jones answers these and others who disagree with her by observing that Martin Luther King, Jr., and Malcolm X spoke and wrote eloquent standard English.

TALKING, LISTENING, WRITING

4. You might ask: "When is the last time you were laughed at because of something you said?"

5. You might start discussion by inviting comments on President Clinton's Southern style, Ross Perot's Texas accent, Henry Kissinger's accent, etc.

6. People "shift gears" based on assumptions they make about their listeners. Few students would answer "Yo, bro" when getting a call from the dean.

PROJECTS

7. In August Wilson's play, for instance, the preacher speaks a language colored by the language of the Bible.

Toni Cade Bambara, "The Lesson"   534

"The Lesson" is the story of the collision of two worlds; the collision occurs when a group of impoverished tough-talking black children are taken to F. A. O. Schwartz and to Fifth Avenue. It is an unlikely setting for a collective epiphany, but there the children learn something about the division of wealth in the world.

THE RESPONSIVE READER

1. Sylvia, who narrates the story, uses profanity when she describes her environment (*pissed, stank, boring ass*), when she speaks of Miss Moore, and, less often, when she speaks of her peers. Is the profanity a defiant rejection of sentimentality and euphemisms that might be used to gloss over the harsh realities of these young people's lives?

2. Key features of the black dialect are omitting the possessive marker ("Junebug foot"), no special verb form for the third person singular indicative ("Miss Moore say," "he *don't* need it"), and deleting the linking verb *to be* ("so we ready," "we a bunch"). The style is sarcastic (as in the mention of the junk man and his horse, for example), and fast-moving (sentences begin with *and, but,* and *so*).

3. College-educated Miss Moore, with her "proper speech," is in the story as a model of black success who challenges Sylvia and the others to look without illusion at their world. "Where we are is who we are," she asserts and adds that it does not "have to be that way." The world can be changed for the better once the poor "wake up and demand their share of the pie." While Sylvia's original smart-alec reaction to Miss Moore makes her out to be a tedious schoolmarm, it becomes evident that Miss Moore is well worth listening to if Sylvia is to do anything unusual or unpredictable with her life?

4. At the toy store the group learns that people exist who have so much money they can spend huge amounts on toys. Sylvia says of such people,

"What kinda work they do and how they live and how come we ain't in on it?" Sylvia personally feels a funny sense of shame at the store's entrance, and this is unsettling to a girl who had hitherto barged through life. After the group returns home the discussion that occurs reveals that the experience has irrevocably altered each individual. In a summing up, the members observe the unfair division of wealth that contradicts the idea of democracy. A sobered Sylvia might have made off with four of Miss Moore's dollars, but the amount, and what it can purchase suddenly seem paltry and tainted?

5. Sylvia may be in some way indirectly autobiographical? Since the story pays subtle, backhanded homage to Miss Moore, it may be that Bambara is in some ways harking back to her own emergence from the limitations of her surroundings?

TALKING, LISTENING, WRITING

6. These children are profane, impatient, and rude and might normally be offputting and annoying, but the whole point of the story is to invite us to see the world for the duration through their eyes?

7. Sylvia's tough talk is a defensive strategy in her dangerous, threatening daily environment and in a society that does not value her as a human being?

8. The story dramatizes the point that something is wrong with a society in which a small group of people control obscene amounts of money while a considerably larger group goes unfed, unsheltered, and uncared for.

PROJECTS

9. Sylvia's defiant "ain't nobody gonna beat me at nuthing" is the defiant self-assertion of a young person with many strikes against her. Arrange to have provocative or characteristic responses shared with the class.

THINKING ABOUT CONNECTIONS

Bambara focuses on the way the language of a social group is part of group identity, reinforcing a sense of solidarity and belonging. Jones focuses on how mastering the prestige dialect ideally enables people to transcend the limits of social class.

Marge Piercy, "Simple Song" 542

Piercy's "simple song" shows the poet's gift for bringing into focus a quasi-archetypal pattern of human interaction.

THE RESPONSIVE READER

1. One hopes everyone has encountered another with whom it is "easy to be together." What makes for easy, open, nondefensive, nonthreatening, and nonjudgmental talk? How important is common background or shared interests?

2. "You are just like me" does sometimes evolve into "how strange you are." "Word matches word" in the harmonious early days, but can, at a later stage, turn into "we can never communicate." Easy co-existence can change into a "hard, hard and weary" time together. Early in a new relationship it seems we cannot hear enough about the other, and all information exchanged is interesting and fascinating. Later in a relationship that has cooled or not succeeded we might feel that the other never talks or never stops talking or never talks about anything that is to the point.

3. The poet's answer is that there is not and never will be someone "just like me." Searching for someone just like oneself is an unstable foundation upon which to try to construct a relationship. "We are not different nor alike / But each strange in his leather body." What is necessary to make two different beings relate to one another is openness, responsiveness, for love "cannot outlive / the open hand / the open eye / the door in the chest standing open."

TALKING, LISTENING, WRITING

4. Piercy says we are "sealed in skin," in our leather bodies, to suggest that we are all caught up in our uniquely personal memories, experiences, expectations, and disappointments. Rather than look for ourselves in others, we should learn to celebrate the special essence of each person? All we can do is to reach out our "clumsy hands," trying to connect?

5. The phrase may be a cliché, but it is also a pithy description of one of the basic problems between people.

PROJECTS

6. Encourage students to build on gesture language and body language as well as typical beckoning and rejecting phrases.

THINKING ABOUT CONNECTIONS

The two stories do not so much treat the familiar theme of difficult communication between two cultures as focus on different ways of relating to one's own culture. "Seventeen Syllables" is about a barrier between a sensitive, poetic mother and an insensitive, literal-minded father. In "Everyday Use," one obstacle to communication is the gap between the would-be sophisticated and politically correct city person and the down-home part of the family closer to their roots.

CHAPTER 10

VIOLENCE: Living at Risk 549

To assure the safety of life and limb is one of the most basic objectives of civil society. Thomas Hobbes in his *Leviathan* (1651) identified as the overriding political imperative the need to declare a truce in the fratricidal war of all against all and to get individuals and groups to give up their arms. Measured by such fundamental criteria, modern society seems to be backsliding rather than making progress. By the same token, as violence escalates, a chorus of warning and pleading voices promotes a range of contradictory or mutually exclusive remedies.

Student Editorial

Steven Musil, "Emotions Clouding Rational Decisions" 551

A week after the murderer of his friend Dennis was sent to prison, Steven Musil writes "an open letter to a lost friend." He tries to maintain a rational, civilized stance when confronted with the eruption of irrational violence.

THE RESPONSIVE READER

1. The case acts out an eerily familiar scenario of irreducible brutal fact and unavailing theory and rationalization. Dennis was shot to death (first shot into the back of his head, two more shots in the face after he fell) with a sawed-off .22-caliber rifle two and a half years before the letter was written. His killer, Tony, who was a coworker, needed money "to cover some debts." Tony killed Dennis while robbing the restaurant of $1,600. The money was recovered in Tony's apartment, and Tony was sentenced to life in prison without the possibility of parole. Dennis was married and had no children. The coroner theorized that Dennis probably "died instantly without suffering." Tony excused his actions by testifying he "was in a cocaine-induced trance," and Musil excuses the absences of coworkers on the anniversary of Dennis' death by noting that many of them no longer work at the restaurant "and are hard to get ahold of."

2. For the writer the letter is an exorcism of sorts? The reader encounters the facts of the murder, the tribute to the victim ("You were so young. So nice, so gentle"), the immediate reactions of friends and co-workers, and the delayed reaction of the author. The reader can empathize with the piety of the closing lines ("Know that we haven't forgotten you just because we are going on with our lives") and can appreciate the wrenching ironies ("The night before you died you said you said that it was time to have a child"). The writer makes a superhuman effort not "to make irrational

decisions" motivated by anger at the killer? He classifies the support of some for the death penalty and gun control with support "for other related causes."

TALKING, LISTENING, WRITING

3. Conservative readers may be less understanding or forgiving of Tony, of cocaine, and of sawed-off shotguns than the writer and the jury. Liberal readers may be thinking in terms of substance abuse prevention or rehabilitation and more effective restrictions on firearms.

4. Somewhat of a loaded question.

5. Local "tragedies" like the one treated in this editorial may trigger indignation and involvement, but do they tend to generate long-range initiatives or corrective action?

6. You may want to ask students to think of this as a "letter to the editor" for a student publication.

PROJECTS

7. Victim's rights advocates have accomplished the precedent of allowing survivors to testify during the penalty phase of a trial and have been working at the often futile task of securing reparations from either the perpetrator or society.

Nan Desuka, "Why Handguns Must Be Outlawed"   554

By all accounts, a majority of the population supports more effective gun control. But it finds itself consistently defeated by a small minority of gun enthusiasts quoting the Second Amendment.

THE RESPONSIVE READER

1. After a dramatic diagnosis of the gun problem in her opening paragraph, Desuka heads straight for the remedy: She seems to have no faith in piddling halfway measures but advocates the outlawing of handguns, with exceptions only for the police.

2. Desuka does a determined, systematic job on the half-truth of slogans. "Guns don't kill people—criminals do" and "We have a crime problem in this country, not a gun problem" are two slogans Desuka attacks. She explains that most people who kill with handguns are not criminals: "Only about thirty percent of murders are committed by robbers or rapists." The other killers are drinking buddies getting into a quarrel, husbands or lovers killing women in a stupid rage, shopkeepers firing at a robber and killing a bystander, kids playing with their macho father's gun, and so on ad nauseam.

The second slogan is used "to mislead, used to direct attention away from a national tragedy." That tragedy is expressed in the statistics of mayhem and homicide: "Conservative estimates" are that handguns annually are used to murder 15,000 Americans, wound over 100,000 more, and accidentally kill at least another 3,000. "There is a crime problem," but there is also a gun problem.

3. Using conservative estimates underscores the magnitude of the problem, and using conservative sources (the FBI, a vice president at Smith and Wesson) makes for a more persuasive argument, and Desuka does both. She uses statistics to buttress the seriousness of her argument, e.g., "for every burglar who is halted by the sight of a handgun, four innocent people are killed by handgun accidents."

4. Desuka acknowledges that the constitutional argument is a persuasive one. However, the Constitution specifically allows an armed and "well-regulated militia," but that does not apply to handgun owners, since they are not members of such an organization (and it is exactly the lack of regulation that is the issue.) Additionally, Desuka's proposal to ban handguns would not "deprive citizens of their rifles or other long-arm guns." Gun control laws have already been found to be constitutional and this precedent renders the "constitutional argument" moot.

TALKING, LISTENING, WRITING

5. Desuka's strongest cards are her harrowing statistics and her convincing array of fumblers and impulse killers?

6. The NRA is an extremely well-organized, well-funded, alert, and persistent lobby on the federal, state, and local government level, which targets opponents in well-organized campaigns.

7. Proposed initiatives may include waiting periods, registration, regulation of applications, and training of gun users (analogous to driver training). A massacre in a Stockton schoolyard led to some bans on assault weapons, while the Brady Bill sought to control (but not ban) handguns.

8. On this topic tempers flare, with "gun nuts" squaring off against "bleeding-heart liberals." Is there such a thing as rational discussion on this topic?

PROJECTS

9. What is the proportion of knifings, poisonings, car bombings, and the like compared with gun-related crimes?

Mike Royko, "Shooting Holes in Gun Laws"   559

Is it a measure for how jaded the American public has become that a columnist needs to dramatize the case of a woman who was the victim of two consecutive rapes in order to make his readers rethink women's need for protection?

THE RESPONSIVE READER

1. Royko is the kind of hands-on journalist to whom a drastic incident is worth a barrel of theories and statistics. After he stimulates the reader's outrage at the incident, Royko concludes that the woman should have been carrying a weapon hidden in her purse, and that she should not have been in violation of the law for doing so. "It doesn't make much sense" that the law allows guns to be kept in the home but does not allow a woman "in a dangerous neighborhood" to carry a concealed pistol. Royko believes in proper registration, in a cooling-off period before purchase, and in keeping machine guns out of the hands of juveniles. But he encourages women to carry guns designed to ward off "thugs" and "two-legged animals."

TALKING, LISTENING, WRITING

2. Some possible cavils: Royko does not say how the woman would fare in a shootout if the rapist also had a gun. As the Goetz case and others showed, where the right to self-defense begins is a thorny question.

3. Remind students that a "rebuttal" requires some systematic argument, not shouting an opponent down as a redneck, a fascist, a racist, or the like.

4. Have students share with the class the best or most provocative of the "columnist-for-a-day" efforts.

PROJECTS

5. Millions every day read the opinions of a favorite columnist—for amusement, for advice, for validation of favorite opinions?

THINKING ABOUT CONNECTIONS

Royko is very good at stimulating gut feelings. The common denominator is the desire to assure the safety of ordinary citizens?

Wendy Kaminer, "Federal Offense"   562

Kaminer's cogently argued essay on the recent stampede toward life sentences for repeat offenders reflects her belief in the capacity of an educated citizenry for rational discussion of an emotion-charged issue.

THE RESPONSIVE READER

1. Kaminer's perspective on "the politics of crime control" is that crime policy in this country is the result of extrapolation from statistics, i.e., "a simple matter of arithmetic." Because there are "more crime victims than criminal defendants, particularly among the voting public," the result is "more conservatives than liberals on the subject of crime—many more." Thus crime victims vote for politicians who will advocate the harshest measures possible for criminals. The resulting legislation reflects the fears of crime victims far more than it acknowledges mitigating circumstances for the criminal. Eighty percent of Americans support the death penalty (absent the option of life without parole), and "this in turn suggests that nearly 80 percent of Americans fear being murdered more than they fear being convicted of murder." The idea that prisons should rehabilitate prisoners was a progressive and humane alternative to the stocks, the lash, or any eye-for-an-eye type of physical punishment. Retribution is more reflective of the zeitgeist (and as old as the hills) and is designed to make the criminal "pay for" his crimes. "Permanent exile" removes undesirable elements to the gulag archipelago of a prison system that is in effect another country.

2. One major weakness of the "three-time-loser" laws is that they do not take into account the nature of the crime committed or the circumstances of the criminal. In one state, for instance, "drunk driving, promoting prostitution, and petty theft" all qualify as "violent" crimes, which are then added to a criminal's total. Another weakness is that "the early release of violent felons," which such laws were supposed to address, continues to occur because prisons are overcrowded with drug offenders serving mandatory sentences. Among the unanticipated results of such laws "may be an increase of violence on the streets: preliminary anecdotal reports from the police suggest that when cornered, offenders may shoot their way out rather than surrender and face life in prison." Furthermore, these laws "are bound to increase the number of trials, since people aren't likely to plead to life imprisonment, resulting in still more delays throughout the system." The nation's prisons and courts will be even more unmanageable as felons demand jury trials where once they might have agreed to a plea bargain.

3. The liberal position is that a criminal is "made, not born, and can sometimes be unmade, if intervention comes early enough." There are "identifiable, treatable connections" between the creation of a criminal and the society from which the criminal emerged. Neglected and abused children who attend ground-zero schools in the inner city, who have no prospects of well-paid employment except as couriers of illegal drugs, and who have no stake in or optimism about society, are frequently and not surprisingly lost to the criminal netherworld. Liberals believe that ameliorating such conditions would lead to a reduction in the number of criminals: "Along with faith in the curative powers of good government, programs to treat and prevent violent behavior reflect faith in the malleability of human beings and the capacity of distressed people and communities for self-improvement." Summing up the conservative position, Ronald Reagan asserted that "There are no social solutions to crime . . . because crime is not a social problem." Instead, crime is "a problem of the human heart."

The conservatives' "bleak vision" of crime is one in which crime is an "unchangeable fact of life." Liberalism is dismissed as "utopian": "Government can respond to the symptoms with arrest and incarceration, but only God can treat the disease." Conservatives believe in the deterrent effect of punishment. In the conservative scenario, criminals are "essentially rational human beings who would be deterred from committing crimes when the associated costs became impractical." Liberals counter that most criminals "never get past assuming they won't be arrested."

4. When Kaminer describes the effects of "mandatory minimum sentences for various drug and firearms offenses," she also presents glimpses of individual human beings affected by these laws. A twenty-four-year-old man is currently "serving ten years in a federal prison because he agreed to help a federal undercover agent find someone selling LSD at a Grateful Dead concert." Another man is "serving five years for a first offense—growing marijuana at home." A judge is quoted regarding the "pathetic cases" that will never be systematically and consistently handled. "No one will ever formulate a system of law for which you don't have to have exceptions," the judge says. He relates the story of "a man with the IQ of a seven-year-old who got a toy gun, went to a bank, got seventy dollars to get an operation for his dog, his best friend in the world, turned himself in to the FBI, and the dog died anyway. What should we do? Give him life?"

5. Mitigating circumstances should again play a part in sentencing criminals: "We want our acts to be judged in the context of motivation and personal history, and a concept of character that involves more than our worst offenses." We must bear in mind that "People do sometimes commit bad acts for good reasons, which means that guilt—and especially sentences—ought to be determined by considering the actor as well as the act." Kaminer further implies that mandatory sentencing laws ought to be scrapped. "If Congress were genuinely interested in truth in sentencing, it would make clear to the public how erratically and arbitrarily mandatory minimums are enforced." Congress should acknowledge that "federal sentencing guidelines already call for very tough sentences for serious crimes," and should admit that mandatory minimum laws are the result of hysterical overreaction. Kaminer would return to judges "limited discretion to vary their sentences."

TALKING, LISTENING, WRITING

6. Encourage candid personal testimony here.

7. Kaminer argues that if the third conviction sends a criminal to jail for life, with no possibility of parole, then all three convictions should be for truly violent felonies. Kaminer would not count drunk driving, pandering, petty theft, and drug possession offenses as violent.

PROJECTS

8. How much of Kaminer's predictions and Cassandra-type warnings are coming true?

Michael Ryan, "I Refuse to Live in Fear"   571

In a mere two newspaper columns, Michael Ryan tells the story of a truly amazing octogenarian who is trying to practice charity and forgiveness in a violent and unforgiving world.

THE RESPONSIVE READER

1. On August 30, 1992, eighty-year-old Eileen Egan was mugged as she walked along the Upper East Side of Manhattan. Her attacker, thirty-year-old Richard Raimonde, attempted to steal Egan's purse, throwing her to the ground in the process. Egan suffered seven broken ribs, a broken hip, and a cut head, and spent the year following the mugging using a walker and a wheelchair. Two years after the attack, Egan told Ryan that she has completely forgotten about it: "I used to get nervous when somebody came up behind me, but that's gone now." Right after the attack, Egan says that she "felt anger," but in the intervening years that anger has been replaced by compassion. Raimonde was "arrested and convicted of second-degree assault. He was sentenced to 3½ to 7 years in prison." Egan was not allowed to speak at Raimonde's sentencing. Raimonde has served his sentence at several of New York State's prisons, including Riker's Island, Elmira, Auburn, and Fishkill. While at Auburn, Raimonde enrolled in a welding class. Egan has communicated with Raimonde via the prison chaplains, and has also communicated with Raimonde's parents.

2. Egan's passion is the desire to dissuade people from lives of criminality and violence. In Egan's words, "If somebody has chosen a life of violence and doesn't get the result he expected from his victim, it may help him to see life differently." Egan believes, "the neediest people of all are those who believe in the efficacy of violence," and as a result she has responded to what she perceives are Raimonde's needs. "I looked at my attacker as a human being," Egan says, "a limited human being. I don't want to push him further down. I'd rather raise him up, so he can take care of himself." Had Egan been allowed to speak at Raimonde's sentencing, she would have said he "is worthy of our respect." Egan quotes from a Hindu writing in response to Ryan's question "if trying to help her attacker had accomplished anything." "It's the action, not the fruit of the action, that's important," Egan quotes. "It may not be in your power, may not be in your time, that there'll be any fruit. But that doesn't mean you stop doing the right thing. You may never know what results come from your action. But if you do nothing, there will be no result."

3. Egan lives in a New York apartment, "filled with books and simple furniture," indicating a "life devoted more to making a difference in society

128

than to making money." Unusual for a woman born around 1912, Egan graduated from college with a degree in English. Subsequently, she "embarked on a career of helping refugees," and as a result of this relief work, she "formed strong views about herself and the world." "Her deep Catholic faith played a prominent part in her thinking."

TALKING, LISTENING, WRITING

4. A good test question for idealists, pragmatists, self-styled "hard-nosed" realists, and just plain cynics.

5. Encourage students to adduce anecdotal evidence from their own experience.

6. How much opposition is there to punitive laws? Where do the churches or other religious institutions stand on the matter?

7. Encourage free and open discussion of the pro and con.

Larry Heinemann, "Tour of Duty"   574

Larry Heinemann, in "Tour of Duty," contrasts the Vietnam War with other wars in terms of emotional responses, induction, demobilization, and the experience of fighting. "War is hell," William T. Sherman said, but Heinemann's essay seems to imply that some types of hell are more diabolical than others.

THE RESPONSIVE READER

1. The two world wars are introduced to establish the continuity of the psychological and emotional trauma war causes, and to show how the induction, fighting, and demobilization unique to the Vietnam War exacerbated that trauma. World War II soldiers "trained together and shipped overseas together," remained soldiers for the duration of the war, and had a longer hiatus between the cessation of fighting and the arrival home than did soldiers in Vietnam; these differences are "crucial."

2. The Vietnam War was "the ugliest, most grueling, and most spiritless work" these soldiers had ever done. A survivor has endured "firefights and ambushes," which are "bloody and nasty, businesslike massacres with meat all over everything," in addition to "jungle rot, heat exhaustion, crabs and head lice, and an endless diarrhea." Then, approximately twenty-four hours after a soldier's tour of duty is up, he rejoins civilian life, a life in which virtually no one understands the nightmare from which he has just emerged. Given these circumstances, it is not surprising that veterans have had a rough transition back to their former lives, if they have been able to make the transition at all.

3. The one-year tour of duty began with Basic Training and Advanced Individual Training before soldiers were shipped overseas. After arriving in Vietnam, a survivor went through the arduous transformation from a dazed newcomer, exhausted by the heat and dangerous to others in his ignorance, to an experienced and tough soldier-specialist who performs with routine coolness "in the midst of an alien ease." The membership of the company is in a constant state of flux as members are killed, wounded, or demobilized. Five days of rest and recuperation in Thailand or Japan are included, but throughout his tour a soldier cares about nothing except finishing his assigned time. The ending date for the tour of duty is what keeps the soldiers going.

4. Heinemann maintains the historical perspective that keeps his account from being one individual's outpouring of personal grievances and traumas, and he frequently checks his own experiences against those of others?

TALKING, LISTENING, WRITING

5. The impulse to blot out and forget militates against the urge to reconsider, to rethink, and to commemorate? Note the way the media periodically revisit the great traumatic moments in American history.

6. The use of profanity in the context of the war experience may be seen as an expression of the refusal to cover up horrible realities with euphemisms and circumlocutions.

7. What are some of the ways people come to terms or cope with traumatic events?

8. Some students may argue for total separation between the military and education; others may insist that students should be able to assess and choose all options.

PROJECTS

9. A possible focus: the treatment of the Vietnam veteran in Hollywood movies. Another possible focus: the national debate about the original Vietnam memorial, the added tribute to the women serving in Vietnam, and the new memorial to the veterans of the "forgotten" Korean War dedicated in 1995.

SUGGESTIONS FOR LANGUAGE WORK

Terms for dictionary work: *sympathetic, trivialize, esprit, reverberate, culinary, benign, claustrophobic, maelstrom, residual, anesthetize.*

"Cambodian Boys Don't Cry" is the eyewitness report of a young boy who witnessed the "killing fields" of Cambodia and whose father, grandfather, sister, and many close relatives perished in the Cambodian holocaust.

THE RESPONSIVE READER

1. Many have tried to visualize what it must feel like to have the steamroller of modern war roll over one's community, bringing death and destruction to familiar, cherished surroundings, like the clustered villages and the "irregular checkerboard" of the rice paddies of Rasmey's childhood. What is hard to imagine is the experience of genocide—a whole population reduced to less than animals, starving women and children worked to death or shot when unable to go on, millions of people destroyed by an ideology gone mad. It is hard to remember that soldiers dehumanized by the power of the gun were once also someone's son, cousin, nephew.

2. The artless candid style of the writer's unfiltered testimony perhaps gives more power to his account than a carefully manipulated media product could. When the narrator describes the abrupt end to his boyhood, he reports feeling ominous premonitions ("My body suddenly started to chill") and fear ("I was nervous and panicked through the whole event"). In describing the events after the Khmer Rouge took control of the country, Rasmey seems at times reticent (or numb?) about his feelings. His account of his brief eery reunion with his mother ("I was shocked; my heart began to pound inside of me") is the closest he comes to being overwhelmed by his feelings?

TALKING, LISTENING, WRITING

3. Historians can no doubt identify contributing factors that all make sense taken by themselves: the rebellion against French colonialism, the exposure of young Indochinese students studying in Paris to the Marxist analysis of bourgeois society as the mortal enemy of workers and peasants, American intervention as the result of the "contain-communism" cold-war mentality, the brutalizing effect of years of jungle warfare and saturation bombing.

4. American policies, however rationalized or condemned, were lethally implicated in the fate of this writer and of millions of others in Southeast Asia. Many Americans have felt a special responsibility for refugees from this part of the world?

PROJECTS

5. Survivors of genocide—Primo Levi, Elie Wiesel, or Dith Pran —remember the nightmarish daily battle to survive, often suffer from post-traumatic stress and survivor's guilt, and want the world to learn what each endured and to make certain such suffering is never allowed to occur again.

Luis Valdez, *The Buck Private (Soldado Razo)* 583

The Buck Private is a starkly simple morality play about the Vietnam War, with macabre comic touches as Death alternately chats or jests with us and sends a shudder down our spines.

THE RESPONSIVE READER

1. Death is the storyteller of *The Buck Private,* unseen by the actors except for one brief occasion. He provides the stage directions, introduces the players, and narrates their inner thoughts. Among people naive about the war and the soldier's impending fate, he is the one who knows. And he makes sure we know. The family is stereotypically unsuspecting or naive (Mother bustling in with a bowl of tamales, little brother blurting out his thoughts) and predictable in their beliefs (Cecilia hoping Johnny is in uniform when they get married, the father celebrating his son's "going to war").

2. Death looks at Johnny's brother and says, "in three or four years, I take him the way I took Johnny. Crazy, huh?" The subtext in much of the play is that minorities with no real prospects for higher education or lucrative careers supply much of the personnel for Uncle Sam's army. At the end of the play the most powerful political statement is made by Johnny's last letter: Johnny writes about the "wasting" of civilians identified by the army with the enemy—"an old man and an old lady," "a small boy about seven years old," and the boy's mother. All the villagers "were supposed to be V-C, communists." But in the dreams of the young Chicano soldier, he looks again at the civilians he had just killed, and they were "my pa, my little brother and you, Mother."

3. The play has a universal appeal, evoking memories of all soldiers who ever awaited shipment overseas, all mothers who had to watch them go, and all surviving fiancées, parents, and siblings?

4. The macabre humor in the play comes from the role of Death ("How goes it, bro?") as mastermind and ironic commentator on the action. He introduces us with lethal irony to the "courageous young men" and to the "beloved mothers" and crying girlfriends they leave behind as they head for the carnage of war. The mother is "a picture of tenderness" who is naively proud that her son has become a man because he has put on a uniform. The little brother's plan to "join the service and get really drunk" when he reaches seventeen. Death is also irreverently funny as he fussily applies make-up (the pale mask of death?) to Johnny and hustles him to his doom. Death here is somewhat of a prankster as well as the grim reaper; he allows us at least to see the grim humor in the absurdity of the situation?

TALKING, LISTENING, WRITING

5. Death says of Johnny (and, by extension, the others): "It never crossed his mind to refuse. How can he refuse the government of the United States? How could he refuse his family?"

6. Have students had actual contact with groups like Beyond War?

7. You may want to warn against ready-made dutiful sentiments.

PROJECTS

8. Experimenting with the deceptively simple, apparently naive Teatro Campesino style can be an educational experience for students.

CHAPTER 11

ENVIRONMENT: Participating in Nature   603

Through millennia, the advance of civilization meant cutting down the virgin forests, bringing the plow to the prairies and steppes, exterminating the animals of the wild, and digging in the bowels of the earth for ore to smelt and fossil fuels to burn. Only slowly have human beings learned the price in erosion and desertification that future generations pay for a heedless exploitation of the natural environment. During the last few centuries, the dizzying pace of technological advance has changed the surface of the planet, obliterated age-old ecosystems, and endangered the ability of Planet Earth to sustain life. How do different cultural traditions envision the relation between civilization and nature? How strong is the "back-to-nature" impulse in our society today?

John (Fire) Lame Deer and Richard Erdoes, "Listening to the Air"   605

Have other cultures had a different, more reverential, relationship to the natural environment that sustains life? "To us, life, all life, is sacred," John (Fire) Lame Deer says in "Listening to the Air." In this selection, he dramatizes the extent to which our modern technological civilization has removed us from nature.

THE RESPONSIVE READER

1. Putting ourselves back in touch with nature requires first of all getting back in touch with our own atrophied senses. Lame Deer advises us to sit directly upon the earth without the accoutrements of modern life—so that we can again feel the grass, the ground, the "yielding shrubs." He encourages us to "think and feel like animals" while we relearn to breathe and smell and hear the life-giving air.

2. The author's indictment of our civilization centers on our despoiling of the land and our arrogant tampering with the animal kingdom. We "have raped and violated" the lands and insulted them with abominations like "missile silos and radar stations." We have "changed the animals" from buffalo, antelope, wolf, coyote (animals with "spiritual, magic power") to placid cows, goats (which will eat your newspaper), and freaks like poodles and lap dogs. It may not be realistic to think that seventy million families could hunt wild birds or leave their "boxes" for "a hot sweat bath" followed by a plunge into a cold stream. But many in the modern world are seeking ways to reconnect with their natural roots.

3. What has happened to the buffalo and coyote mirrors what has happened to Native Americans. This is Lame Deer's closing statement: "They are treating coyotes almost as badly as they used to treat Indians."

TALKING, LISTENING, WRITING

4. We often seem to be caught in the paradox that bringing people back to unspoiled nature results in the despoiling of the visited sites?

5. Somewhat of a leading question—however, the symbiotic relationship between humans and their dogs and livestock has been a major factor in the survival of the human species.

6. The more "realistic" or hard-nosed people are on this kind of question, the less need they will feel for soul-searching and "white guilt" on this subject?

PROJECTS

7. Anthropologists and linguists have long labored to record and examine what remains of the tremendous linguistic and cultural range of the Native American peoples. Certainly the last quarter of the twentieth century has been a time of preservation and reclamation of Native American heritage and culture?

Marie De Santis, "Last of the Wild Salmon"   610

To De Santis, the life cycle of the wild salmon with its incredible, arduous final journey back to the spawning grounds is a marvelous symbolic reenactment of the vital forces or energies that sustain life. At the same time, our human meddlesomeness threatens to make the salmon runs impossible, leaving us with artificially bred salmon from fish farms, no more like a real salmon than a poodle is to its cousins of the wild.

THE RESPONSIVE READER

1. The author's description of the struggle of the salmon upstream becomes a tribute to the indomitable force that enables life on this planet to survive against odds. At the beginning, the salmon is wounded, tattered, exhausted, and it appears on the verge of death. The animal's powerful primeval instinct to return to the stream of its birth overrides the exhaustion: "the urge and will and passion ignores the animal body and focuses on the stream." Somehow the salmon persists against the stream, and continues on the journey "that brings life to meet death at a point on a perfect circle."

2. In this account, the successive stages of the life cycle assume mythical significance. After the salmon are born, they travel toward the sea. In an extraordinary transformation, the formerly fresh water fish prepare to enter the ocean. The salmon's life after it enters the sea "remains one of the most mysterious on earth." When the urge to spawn arrives, the salmon goes back to the estuary from which it originally entered the sea, converts back to a fresh water fish, and prepares to return "to the exact gravel-bedded streamlet of its birth." The salmon fasts on its journey against the current and yet successfully scales "hurtling waterfalls" or "vertical rocks up to 60 feet high." The exhausted fish chooses a mate, and upon arrival the pair fend off intruders, ready a nest, and spend two to three days releasing eggs and sperm. After all the eggs have been "thrown," the salmon "lies by the nest and dies."

TALKING, LISTENING, WRITING

3. That the salmon returns to the place of its birth to give life before dying reaffirms the principle of symmetry, of things moving in a cycle, eventually returning to their origins. (A different perspective might make us focus on life cut short, aborted, or working at cross purposes?)

4. Butterflies, for instance, undergo incredible metamorphoses.

5. In the nineteenth century, studies of the life cycles of dominant civilizations—their rise and decline—were fashionable. Corporate history may chronicle the slow evolution from the unorthodox initiatives of maverick founders to the gradual hardening of the bureaucratic arteries and to the ascendancy of timid timeservers.

PROJECTS

6. For instance, this country has had some success in cleaning Lake Erie, and the English have had some success with cleaning the Thames River?

TALKING ABOUT CONNECTIONS

Reverence for life and suspicion of human attempts to tamper with nature may prove a strong common thread.

Judi Bari, "The Feminization of Earth First!"   614

Judi Bari, "a lifelong activist," joined Earth First!, an environmental group dedicated to saving the redwoods, and was very nearly killed for her efforts. In this essay, sexual politics changes environmental politics (as it tends to change any other kind of politics). The group changed from one dominated by men who committed "individual acts of daring" to one with seventy-five percent of its leaders as female community activists.

THE RESPONSIVE READER

1. Bari's description of one-thousand-year-old trees so immense that one fills "an entire logging truck" and of "six-inch-diameter baby trees" being logged to "pay off corporate junk bonds" is likely to hit a nerve with even minimally environmentally sensitive readers. So is her picture of the "miles and miles of clearcuts" where there was once a living forest.

2. Earth First! men were known as "no compromise" ecologists who would place themselves "in front of the bulldozers and chain saws to save the trees." Their philosophy was that "the Earth is not just here for human consumption." All this, and the fact that "they played music" and were "funny and irreverent," attracted Bari to their cause. However, the invisibility among the leadership of the hard-working women of the movement, the image of "big man goes into big wilderness to save big trees," and the absence of "community-based organizing" are limitations of Earth First! that Bari criticizes.

3. Logging of redwoods is dominated by a few big timber corporations. The impoverished communities in the northwest timber country all "bow to the economic blackmail of King Timber." Bari sees the corporations as thugs who ruin the environment for profit, enslave timber workers in company towns, and use violence to combat peaceful protest. She is more sympathetic to the workers and speaks of building alliances "with progressive timber workers" that unite both groups "against the big corporations."

4. Bari organized the local community and "planned logging blockades around local issues." Feminization meant that women became a visible part of Earth First!'s persona, that more members were women and families from the community, and that the leadership was eventually seventy-five percent female after the "Redwood Summer." Bari details "specifically misogynist" death threats, hate letters, and the bomb attack. To her, these seemed far more concerned with targeting women in the movement—"whores, lesbians, and members of NOW"—than with opposition to ecological movements dedicated to saving trees.

TALKING, LISTENING, WRITING

5. Does the term *radical* still scare, or scare off, today's students? The basic rationale of a radical stance is that genteel tut-tutting merely salves the protester's conscience?

6. A very basic question.

7. Clean water, clean air, less burning of fossil fuels, doing without nuclear power, stopping off-shore drilling, cleanup of toxic sites, weaning Americans from dependence on the automobile, and saving endangered species are among the many conflicting priorities. (You may want to list these on the chalkboard for discussion and ranking by the class.)

PROJECTS

8. Weeks after front-page newspaper coverage accused Bari of being the creator and transporter of the bomb that went off in her car, a small article appeared in the back pages that said that charges against her had been dropped. Karen Silkwood, a worker at a Kerr-Magee plutonium reprocessing plant, died in a suspicious car crash. She was on the verge of presenting health, safety, and security violations at the plant to the news media.

Charles Krauthammer, "Saving Nature, But Only for Man"   619

Krauthammer is one of many conservative journalists who thrive on exposing and deploring what they consider the excesses of the radical left. At the same time, his columns illustrate how much of what was once considered radical has become part of the "me-too" stance of a "neo-conservative" right. This essay argues that "Nature is our ward" and should be conserved insofar as such conservation protects "the health and safety of people."

THE RESPONSIVE READER

1. Sane environmentalism distinguishes between environmental "luxuries" and environmental "necessities," and we should be solely concerned with the latter. Top priority should be any environmental problem that "directly threatens the health and safety of people." Such pragmatic environmentalism is the only program "that will win universal public support." The test cases the writer offers are ozone depletion and the greenhouse effect, both of which "directly threaten man," with potentially staggering consequences. If the ozone effect proves a reality, flooded coastal cities and parched plains that were once breadbaskets will be the result. A sane environmentalism would concentrate all its energies to ensure man's survival. "Nature is here to serve man" is Krauthammer's anthropocentric claim.

2. Sentimental environmentalism asks us to make sacrifices for other creatures (such as snail darters and caribou) and views the earth as in need of protection against and preservation from our despoiling human activities. Krauthammer responds that humankind preserves nature "on the grounds of self preservation." He quotes Protagoras' maxim: "Man is the measure of all things." The spotted owl is an aesthetic pleasure to contemplate, but preserving the owl is not worth "the loss of livelihood for 30,000 logging families."

TALKING, LISTENING, WRITING

3. Some considerations for those who write in rebuttal: One person's necessity is another person's luxury? Activities with short-range benefits for humans—strip mining, clear-cutting of trees—contribute to a long-range degradation of the environment?

PROJECTS

4. Global warming has been the subject of much discussion but little action. The worldwide environmental summit held in 1992 in Rio de Janeiro produced many paper pledges but also stubborn dissent.

Vicki Hearne, "What's Wrong with Animal Rights"   622

In "What's Wrong with Animal Rights," Vicki Hearne defends animal trainers against the "skewed value system" of the animal rights movement.

THE RESPONSIVE READER

1. Animal rights activists, as seen through Hearne's unsympathetic lens, object to the way we make helpless animals serve for our pleasure and the way we torture animals during medical experiments. Hearne counterattacks by charging that animals are ironically most often exterminated by humane societies—devoted to the "Prevention of Cruelty to Animals." Human beings—and in particular trainers and veterinarians—are less cruel to animals than nature is. Captive animals live longer than those in the wild, for example, for the wild is not "a suffering-free zone or all that frolicsome a location."

2. As an animal trainer, Hearne reads into animals the satisfactions that human beings derive from responding to a challenge or from performing a difficult task well. "Work is the foundation for the happiness a trainer and an animal discover together." Hearne has a whole range of examples of animals apparently getting satisfaction from sources other than mere creature comforts: the "joyful length of stride" for the racehorse Secretariat, the "invention and variation" of "chimp vaudevillians," the rhinoceros who is happy being retrained each morning, and the writer's Airedale who learns that there is "a public place where his work is respected." Such satisfaction comes "from something within the animal" and is akin to "the satisfaction felt by a good wood-carver or a dancer or a poet."

3. Paradoxically, while ascribing to animals quasi-human motives and satisfactions, Hearne claims that animals cannot have rights, which imply mutually understood and reciprocal relationships in a context of custom and tradition? Rights are formulated through language and implemented through

institutional mechanisms beyond the reach of animals, whatever their intuitive understanding of nuances of human identity and status.

TALKING, LISTENING, WRITING

4. Many people who spend much time around animals tend to develop a strong sense of mutual understanding?

5. Hearne loves her animals and cares for them in her fashion—in the fashion of the human being using animals strictly for human purposes?

6. Note that the animal rights movement has called into question many customary ways of keeping animals and dealing with them—many practices that until recently most people took for granted?

PROJECTS

7. Note that many such initiatives have built up powerful momentum and become forces for politicians and business executives to reckon with and ignore at their peril.

Letters to the Editor

"Animal Rights, Wronged"   631

Vicki Hearne's article clearly struck a responsive chord, as these letters to the editor attest.

THE RESPONSIVE READER

1. The first letter writer quickly punctures the caricature of the animal rights extremist who wants to have domestic pets "phased out," sarcastically reassuring Hearne that most animal rights activists are "not losing sleep over her playing fetch with her loyal Drummer." The real issue is the ghastly cruelties inflicted on lab animals—"the wanton destruction of laboratory rats to test cosmetics or the obsessive shooting of cats to study gunshot wounds." Unlike the harsh processes of nature, these cruelties are intentionally inflicted for often frivolous purposes.

2. The second writer can see the "very real desire of some animals to please humans." However, the writer turns the tables on Hearne by highlighting the unnatural or grotesque aspects of the animal acts: The draft horse tries to pull "an unbearable weight," and the rhinoceros' routine involves "a tiny stool" and "ballet steps." In the Jeffersonian tradition, this writer assumes that certain moral imperatives are self-evident. "Pouring oven cleaner in rabbits' eyes" is wrong and sickening regardless of whether the law has gotten around to proscribing the practice.

140

3. The third writer maintains that animal training is a euphemism for subduing animals with sadistic cruelty and deprivation. As a result, Hearne, an animal trainer, is not a legitimate spokesperson for animal rights. The writer disputes Hearne's contention that animal captivity is not inherently evil since suffering exists in the wild and captive lions and orangutans live longer in captivity; "even a few natural years in the wild" is better than "a longer lifetime of incarceration, boredom, and 'training.' "

TALKING, LISTENING, WRITING

4. Most of these writers appeal to a basic and commonsensical empathy for suffering, abused fellow creatures?

5. Would your students tend toward a middle-ground position—that testing cosmetics on animals is not defensible but that using animals to test medicine or fight lethal disease is?

6. Encourage candid expression but also "rational" support of a range of views?

PROJECTS

7. Issues like sexual harassment, child abuse, or homeless shelters seem to provide the focus of letters to the editors during different cycles?

Short Story

Farley Mowat, "The Snow Walker"   635

In "The Snow Walker," Mowat tells the story of a boy and a fox who were known as "The Two Who Were One." Their story is one of an intimate, harmonious relation between human beings and nature, which ends as the arrival of white civilization disturbs and destroys the age-old patterns of native life.

THE RESPONSIVE READER

1. Angutna's people lived in an incredibly harsh environment but in harmony with the changing cycle of the seasons. They lived in a camp of tents in a country of lakes, "roaring rivers," "rolling plains and hills," and walls of "looming cliffs." The area had severe winters with great storms, blizzards, and gales, but the people had learned to live through that season, relying on the food stockpiled the previous fall. In the spring the people hunted the returning deer, "and the camps woke to new and vigorous life." When the deer went further north for summer fawning, the people hunted the nesting geese, and when the deer returned on their southern migration, the people spent

autumn stocking food and preparing for winter. The people were thus intimately caught up with the migratory habits of the animals, which in turn were triggered by the change of seasons.

2. Mowat writes about the people of the North with tremendous empathy and affection. Because Angutna believed the fox was a manifestation of the "Spirits-Who-Help," the relationship of the two is enhanced by the spiritual bond that existed between them. Mowat paints with harsh realism the hardships of winter and the hunger when the fall hunt was poor, but he also makes it clear that for the people of the North the arrival of white civilization brought dislocation, poverty, dependency, and disease.

3. Mowat focuses on the material and spiritual upheaval caused by contact with white civilization. Physically the white men brought a disease that killed half the people and panicked most of the survivors into fleeing east because they believed the land to be cursed. A way of life was radically changed from one of self-sufficiency to one in which the men hunted the (increasingly rare) foxes for their pelts; these were then traded for food. The fox hunters and traders learned that the fox was less reliable or self-replenishing than the deer and, as the fur-hunting and trading lifestyle left nothing to fall back upon, the people began to starve. "Rifles, steel knives, copper kettles" at first represented wealth but were ultimately a poor substitute for a natural self-supporting way of life. The traditional courtesy and hospitality of the people disappeared in the face of starvation.

4. The white man is not represented as personally evil but as the agent of the evil that befalls Angutna and his people? The trader tempts the people to abandon the way of life that has sustained them for generations. He is shrewd enough not to push his offer to buy Angutna's fox, and he also is aware that he is an outsider who knows how little he knows about the way the people really think and feel. He can look at "the big, staring eyes and the swollen bellies of Angutna's children," feel pity, yet conclude that he cannot share the food in his storehouse because it belonged to the company and "he could not part with a pound unless there was payment in fur."

TALKING, LISTENING, WRITING

5. Angutna might have said that he was going to sacrifice the fox for the sake of his family—but that it was not a sacrifice he could live with, so he would offer the sacrifice of himself to atone for the offense to his Spirit-Who-Helps.

6. A challenging assignment.

7. The trading post is "a dark place filled with dark thoughts." From a celebration of the continuing seasons and traditions, the people's outlook changes to that of a grim wait for death by starvation. The basic change is from a reverential attitude toward the animals on which the people depend for food to one of large-scale, "commercial" exploitation?

PROJECTS

8. A nationwide referendum, rejected by the Canadian voters, provided among other things for extended autonomy of the people of the North.

THINKING ABOUT CONNECTIONS

Mowat makes his readers think in terms of an idealized symbiotic relationship between human beings and their animals rather than of animals free of meddling interference from humans?

Poem

Gianfranco Pagnucci, "The Death of an Elephant"   646

Elephants are the largest surviving land animals, and their need of a large supportive habitat makes them seem doomed when gophers and rats have better odds for survival.

THE RESPONSIVE READER

1. Mirroring the behavior of humans, the herd engages in a keening ritual when it forms a half moon, "screaming and trumpeting," around the dying elephant. While the young are perplexed by the death and think they can tug or push the elephant out of it, the great bull, who knows the significance of the other elephant's collapse, defiantly and hopelessly tries to revive her. It is as if a human mother had collapsed and her children fearfully tried to wake her up while her husband expressed his anguish by futilely trying to bring her back to life.

TALKING, LISTENING, WRITING

2. Make allowance for a wide range of perspectives here. (The poet seems intent on making us realize that bonding, solidarity, grieving, and eventual resignation are not exclusively human characteristics.)

PROJECTS

3. Note that all the poems listed here project an unusual fascination with and empathy for the animal kingdom.

CHAPTER 12

UNCERTAIN FUTURE: Dream or Nightmare   655

Predicting the future has long been a small-scale industry, with practitioners ranging from augurers, prophets, and clairvoyant readers to trend watchers and economic forecasters. Much thinking about the future in our modern world has been overshadowed by the spectre of nuclear war and by the population explosion that threatens to destroy the ability of the planet to sustain human life. In the more intermediate range, what do informed and concerned Americans see as they gaze into the crystal ball?

Student Editorial

Mary R. Callahan, "Pro-Choice, Not Pro-Abortion"   657

Being pro-choice, says Callahan, does not mean being an advocate of abortion. Rather it means that one supports the right of a woman to make her own choice in a matter with profound repercussions for a woman's life.

THE RESPONSIVE READER

1. Callahan takes her stand in the fourth paragraph when she defines pro-choice as supporting an individual's right to choose whether or not to carry a pregnancy to term. Because the individual must live with the consequences of the decision, because each individual case is different, and because the individual knows what is best for her life, government should refrain from dictating "morality or obligation for the individual." Freedom to make our choices, right or wrong, is the essence of a free society—including the choice to use racial slurs or the choice to grow fat while most of the rest of the world goes hungry. (The government should not involve itself in either even though Callahan finds both "morally repugnant.")

2. In the first sentence of the editorial, Callahan shows she is aware of the debate by indicating she has written on it before and hopes not to do so again! She is responding to a new tactic by the anti-choice groups when she comments on their use of graphic, revolting photographs.

TALKING, LISTENING, WRITING

3. *Roe* v. *Wade* in 1973 extended the right to privacy to include the right to choose and have an abortion. Twenty years later, the Supreme Court had in successive votes circumscribed and watered down that decision (and the justices who continued to support it were close to retirement). Media-effective and well-organized anti-abortion campaigns, abetted by anti-

abortion legislators, are successfully limiting access to abortions regardless of the legalistic contortions of the courts.

4. Maybe yes, maybe no.

5. Anti-abortion groups have in recent years had the upper hand in terms of gut-wrenching descriptions and pictures of the aborted fetus. Pro-choice activists have found it harder to dramatize the plight of unwilling mothers and unwanted children?

PROJECTS

6. A difficult but educational undertaking. One key question in the abortion debate is at what point according to various religious and legal definitions life begins. The medical debate centers on the viability of the fetus to survive outside of the womb, usually defined as after twenty-four weeks?

Philip Elmer-Dewitt, "Bards of the Internet"   660

"Every night," Elmer-Dewitt says, "when they should be watching television, millions of computer users sit down at their keyboards." His essay is one of many probing the effect going on line has on the lifestyles, interaction styles, and writing styles of a new generation.

THE RESPONSIVE READER

1. Before the onset of the computer age, many assumed that the telephone had rendered writing all but obsolete. To be sure, "there were still full-time scribblers" and the "great centers of commerce still found it useful to keep on hand people who could draft a memo, a brief, a press release or a contract," but "most folks took the easy route and gave their fingers—and sometimes their mind—a rest."

2. The greatest effect networking has had on the way people communicate is to move people further away from the pen, and away from the telephone and the television. Instead, people sit down at keyboards, dial up a computer networking service, and improvise fiction and non-fiction, to be read instantly by thousands of readers. The style of writing in the computer age is inextricably linked to the medium used for communication: "Curiously, what works on the computer networks isn't necessarily what works on paper." "Good writing on the Net tends to be clear, vigorous, witty and above all brief," says Elmer-Dewitt, and a Canadian writing teacher concurs, "The medium favors the terse," i.e., "short paragraphs, bulleted lists and one-liners are the units of thought here." The networks charge by the minute; speed is thus critical. Network writing must be thought of as a kind of talk/write: "written speech," a "little more considered than coffeehouse talk and a lot less considered than a letter."

3. The sheer number of computer writers and the anonymity of computer writing makes possible participation way beyond that allowed by the insider-controlled, highly selective print media. Networks are available to anyone who has access to a computer and knows how to type. This type of milieu has "enfranchised thousands of would-be writers who otherwise might never have taken up the craft." In addition, computer writing has "thrown together classes of people who hadn't had much direct contact before: students, scientists, senior citizens, computer geeks, grass-roots (and often blue collar) bulletin-board enthusiasts and most recently the working press."

TALKING, LISTENING, WRITING

4. Allow time for detailed testimonials here?

5. Scheduling, inventory control, and monitoring of employee performance are some of the major areas where the computer is becoming an ever-present element in our lives.

PROJECTS

6. Encourage students to devise questionnaires or protocols that would provide some "hard data" for interpretation.

Lester C. Thurow, "The New Economics of High Tech"   664

Lester Thurow contends that the United States is focusing on an obsolete product technology that leaves it ill prepared for competing with the emphasis on process technology in Japan and Germany

THE RESPONSIVE READER

1. In the next century, the long-term competitive advantage will go to countries that use a new process technology that focuses on faster and cheaper production of goods and services that already exist. Currently, the United States continues to lose ground competitively because it spends two-thirds of research and development money on new products and one-third on process, while the Japanese spend two-thirds of research and development money on process and one-third on product. This means that Japan is good at producing other people's products more quickly and cheaply, thus taking the product—the video recorder, fax, the CD player—"away from the inventor."

2. New-product technology is dedicated to the invention of new products while new-process technology is concerned with producing such "goods and services cheaper, faster, and better." Reverse engineering looks at an existing product and creates a new and better process to manufacture it, in a sequence that is the reverse of the usual procedure. Human resource

allocation is the division of a company's employees among manufacturing, engineering, quality, marketing, and development.

3. American management is top heavy with money manipulators who know little about technology. American chief executive officers rarely rise through the ranks from production, and Thurow contends this trend must be reversed. Seventy percent of European and Japanese CEOs have "technical backgrounds" compared with thirty percent in the United States; this in large part explains the country's repeated failure to "profit from technological advancement." The American steel industry is an excellent example of the decline that inevitably follows the failure to realize and capitalize upon the new process technologies. American companies view labor as "simply another factor of production to be hired"; they spend less money upgrading the skills of these employees than do either Germany or Japan and concentrate that investment on high-level employees; and they do not train workers in "the basic background skills" that will enable them to absorb new technologies. The American education system has heretofore failed to educate the "bottom fifty percent" of the population sufficiently to prepare it for the "new high-tech processes."

TALKING, LISTENING, WRITING

4. Among familiar assorted grievances: Europe and Japan create multifarious obstacles in order to reduce and delay the import of American products; Japan has in the past "dumped" huge quantities of underpriced electronic goods in an effort to capture the market; European and Japanese companies often enjoy substantial government subsidies or less overt support; neither country made comparable sacrifices comparable to the United States' efforts in the Cold War. (Most of these would seem like excuses or alibis to people like Thurow?)

5. Thurow is not completely pessimistic, but he is aware that he is advocating swift and sweeping changes before any turn-around can occur. If these changes are not implemented, Thurow would not be overly hopeful about this country's future?

6. The average voter is unlikely to encounter, let alone to evaluate, arguments like Thurow's in sound-bites, political speeches, or debates?

PROJECTS

7. Note that it may be virtually impossible in this global economy of mergers, pacts, joint ventures, and licensing agreements to buy anything truly created and made exclusively in America.

Garrett Hardin, "Lifeboat Ethics"   669

Hardin became one of the most widely read and heeded of a new breed of "hard-nosed" neoconservatives who scoffed at the idea that America could feed a starving world (and admit much of it to its shores). The central question that Garrett Hardin answers in the negative is: "Does everyone on Earth have an equal right to an equal share of its resources?" Aid to irresponsible nations or governments merely encourages the practices that perpetuate poverty and overpopulation.

THE RESPONSIVE READER

1. If the planet is envisioned as a spaceship, we must all be responsible for everyone's well-being and conserve and share the craft's limited resources. No one has the right to "to destroy, waste, or use" more than one person's allotment of resources. Hardin, on the other hand, calls "suicidal" the idea that everyone in the rest of the world is in the same boat (or ship) with us and therefore has equal claim on our own limited resources.

2. If each rich nation is a lifeboat, it is a boat that floats in the sea of the world's impoverished people. Hardin's point is that we are not all fellow passengers on Spaceship Earth; rather the rich nations of the world are lifeboats and the majority of the world's population is swimming around those boats, desperate to clamber aboard. Hardin uses the lifeboat analogy to support his contention that the rich nations should not let anyone on board for fear the boat will be swamped or its margin of safety compromised. This attitude may be un-Christian and "morally abhorrent" to many, but it is the only policy that will assure the survival of the people in the boat.

3. The *commons* was a medieval system where members of a community all had the right to graze their livestock on the common pasture. Hardin's theory of the "the tragedy of the commons" stipulates that under such a system everyone will use the common resources to the maximum while not feeling responsible for upkeep and conservation—after all, the commons is not "theirs." (Whales were decimated because they were everybody's and nobody's.) "Voluntary restraint" does not work and leads to "mutual ruin."

4. Hardin sees the Green Revolution as a "well-intended humanitarian effort" that, ironically, caused further damage to the environment by sustaining larger populations. Unrestrained population growth will ultimately endanger or destroy everything needed for maintaining the quality of life—"food, air, water, forests, beaches, wildlife, scenery and solitude."

5. Hardin co-opts liberal terminology by talking about safeguarding the environment when he really means safeguarding the privileged lifestyle of the fortunate few? Loaded language like "boarding parties" makes the starving, apathetic multitudes of the Third World sound like Viking pirates?

TALKING, LISTENING, WRITING

6. An exercise that should dramatize for students how key metaphors focus or channel our thinking.

7. An exercise in semantics? Realism sounds self-congratulatory—we are prepared to face facts and reality and dismiss the visionary. Pragmatism sounds more defensive—no matter what our ultimate goals, we have to judge actions or policies by their practical results. Cynicism condemns people who are so excessively realistic as to always expect the worst—in particular, to expect the worst of other human beings?

8. One student said, "An ideal reader would be a conservative who was born into an old-money family and who is carrying on the family's business. A hostile reader would be a liberal from a devout but impoverished family who is struggling to keep his head above water." Is this too simple?

PROJECTS

9. Ironically, the populations of both groups increased faster than Hardin predicted. By 1992, yearly immigration into the United States was predicted to be 600,000 people, of whom one-third enter illegally. Unexpected statistic: In 1992 the United Nations Food and Agricultural Organization reported that the world produces enough to feed everyone and that there were 150 million fewer malnourished people in poorer countries than there were twenty years ago. This development was credited to the "Green Revolution," which improved grain varieties and brought better storage, distribution, and agricultural methods. Bottom line: a thirty-year population growth of 1.8 billion.

SUGGESTIONS FOR LANGUAGE WORK

Terms for dictionary work: *ethics, abhorrent, substantive, reproductive, aggregate, ratio, sovereign, philanthropic, discretion, antagonism.*

Richard Cohen, "Our Children Are Our Future—Unfortunately They're Bigots"   676

Richard Cohen reports on the results of a recent public opinion survey, and what he concludes is disturbing. Is it true that "a generation of bigots is coming of age"?

THE RESPONSIVE READER

1. The traditional assumption about intolerance is that it is inversely proportional to years of schooling. "Opinion polls have always found that the more schooling a person has, the more likely he is to be tolerant." Thus, up until now, "older people—who by and large have the least education" have been "the most intolerant age group in the nation." Reversing this traditional assumption, the survey showed that today "older and younger white Americans share the same biases." Answers to survey questions by people under thirty revealed that young Americans, who have had educational

opportunities that older Americans have not, are almost on par with those older Americans in terms of bigotry and racism. Aside from congenital bigotry and historical ignorance, Cohen does acknowledge that those Americans receiving the most years of education may have been influenced by real or imagined slights as a result of affirmative action in graduate schools and university hiring.

2. Survey test questions Cohen cites: Do blacks prefer to remain on welfare rather than work? do blacks "complain too much about racism?" do blacks "stick together more than others?" "do you feel you have ever been a victim of reverse discrimination in hiring or promotion?" Cohen says the questions are "designed to ferret out biased attitudes," but he acknowledges that "not all of the statements represent proof of bigoted attitudes." A white college student's affirmative response to the question about blacks sticking together could reflect the white student's observance of "voluntary self-segregation on the part of black students," rather than bigotry.

3. Americans under thirty are "pathetically ignorant of recent American history," Cohen says, "Younger people apparently know little about—and did not see on television—the civil rights struggles of the 1950s and 1960s, everything from the police dogs of Birmingham to the murder of civil rights workers." Without such a historical framework, a young person would have no understanding or compassion for the original intent of affirmative action. Furthermore, since affirmative action is a factor in graduate school admissions and in university hiring, some of the highly educated (26 percent of college graduates; 23 percent of post-graduates) answered in the affirmative when asked, "Do you feel you have ever been a victim of reverse discrimination in hiring or promotion?"

TALKING, LISTENING, WRITING

4. Cohen has three suggestions: to teach young Americans the recent history of their country ("It's nothing less than a calamity that a generation has come of age without a deep appreciation of the recent history of African-Americans"); to discourage black leaders from encouraging "self-segregation" ("black leaders who advocate or condone separatism had better appreciate the damage they are doing"); and to re-evaluate the effects of affirmative action ("affirmative action programs, as well-intentioned as they may be, need to be re-examined—and without critics automatically being labeled as racist").

5. The conservative revival of recent years is seen by many as fueled by subliminal racist appeals, while conservatives claim to be aiming at a society that is truly "color-blind."

6. Opportunities for some good "investigative journalism" here.

PROJECTS

7. How trusting or how skeptical should we be about the polling mania that bedevils politicians and policy makers at every step?

Shapiro uses this multiple book review to examine the state of the feminist movement in America at the end of the twentieth century, in a time of stock-taking and second thoughts.

THE RESPONSIVE READER

1. The spirit Shapiro invokes in her introductory paragraph is that of the optimistic explosion of feminism in the 1960s: "Douglas's fluorescent message," (defined in the opening sentence as "The more I see of men, the more I like dogs," and written in paint upon a window) "perfectly captured the spirit of those early years." The spirit was flamboyant, excessive, and with a "hard kernel of truth." The early years were a time when "barriers toppled, new frontiers seemed to open daily; it was exhilarating, it was unstoppable." The key concern Shapiro has is that such spirit has been lost, and the "unstoppable" has in fact been stopped. Despite feminist victories (including "two Supreme Court justices and the first Disney heroine in history who'd rather read than get married"), "complaints about the women's movement are piling up," and the movement itself is divided, contentious, and unfocused. The title is an ironic play on the pioneering feminist book, *Sisterhood Is Powerful.*

2. Victim feminism may be observed at feminist conferences when participants divide themselves into differing groups of victims ("grievance groups"). These groups ("Jewish women, Asian-American women, fat women, old women") can divide into subgroups ("The Jewish women discovered they were deeply divided: some accepted being Jewish; others were seeking to recover from it"), and the group participants sing songs, enjoy "healing rituals," and, no surprise, listen to "victim testimonials." Gender feminism, described as being in "the ascendancy," is a movement "devoted to nurturing femaleness in various treacly ways." "Such phony issues as date rape and self-esteem preoccupy gender feminists," and one of the books Shapiro is reviewing is concerned with how gender feminists are transforming academia: "While male students are off studying . . . engineering and biology, women in feminist classrooms are sitting around being 'safe' and 'honoring' feelings." Equity feminism is succinctly defined as being "dedicated to achieving equal rights."

3. Sherrye Henry's book, *The Deep Divide*, is an attempt to discover how "the current movement beset by radicals" managed to get so "out of touch with ordinary women" and how feminists could concentrate instead on becoming "a movement for women, children and families." Shapiro says: "give Henry credit: she knows the difference between the media-generated monsters of 'women's lib' and the real women's movement." However, Shapiro rejects Henry's calls for "nicely dressed," non-"mannish" women to come and lead the movement away from "icky problems" like lesbian rights, wife battering, and abortion. Shapiro's review of Fleming's book, *Motherhood Deferred,* is sharply critical: Fleming's book describes how Fleming became part of a "sacrificial generation" of women who "put off

pregnancy for work, waiting so long that they lost the chance." Fleming concludes that her own infertility is the result of her feminist labors, and a good portion of her book is devoted to describing her attempts to conceive. Fleming "barely admits the possibility that her infertility might have roots someplace other than her politics," and she could never have been described as a "hapless zombie of the women's movement," judging by the content and titles of some of her earlier feminist writing ("female ethnicity" and "a defense of flirting"). Shapiro's response to Fleming's attempts to have a child are sympathetic ("the sadness of her plight"), but the book "badly misrepresents the women's movement, which did a lot more agitating for day care than issuing decrees against childbearing."

4. Douglas and Steinem are "unrepentant, unreformed feminists" because they "liked the women's movement just fine and still do." Both Douglas and Steinem have been involved in the movement for over twenty-five years, and neither has gotten too sidetracked by issues that may not have tremendous significance for the majority of women. Douglas' book is a "first-rate analysis" of the cultural influences that shaped the 1950s woman. Douglas explores how feminism got "turned into a dirty word" and how the first three simple feminist demands ("equal opportunity for women in employment and education, twenty-four hour child-care centers and abortion on demand") first began to be overshadowed by anything flamboyant the media could focus upon. Although "a lot of ordinary women admire Gloria Steinem," Shapiro implies that it is too bad that Steinem, one of the few feminist leaders palatable to large numbers of people, both male and female, "seems to claim the role of rebel without living it." Shapiro does appreciate Steinem's "fascinating piece about how Ms. Magazine tried to lure traditional women's magazine advertising."

5. Shapiro shows that she is not wholly hostile to feminist radicals by pointing out that "The American women's movement has always had an avante-garde." Shapiro observes that Elizabeth Cady Stanton, exalted by one of the writers reviewed as "the very model of equity feminism," also had a radical side. Stanton "mortified her colleagues in the mid-19th century by demanding divorce rights and terming marriage 'legalized prostitution.'" Gloria Steinem is quoted, "I'm looking forward to trading moderation for excess," which is apparently the path that Stanton followed. By ending on such a note, Shapiro offers optimism for feminism's future.

TALKING, LISTENING, WRITING

6. Students may or may not be willing to take a stand on all three of these.

7. and 8. Ask students to offer supporting evidence for their perceptions.

PROJECTS

9. This may be an opportunity to bring in a faculty member teaching women's issues as a guest lecturer or outside expert.

THINKING ABOUT CONNECTIONS

All of these women are determined to help foster equality in the world, whether in magazine writing, the environmental movement, the justice system, or between generations. Their differences in perspective may be attributed to generational differences and to the different areas in which they have focused their attention. Judi Bari and Naomi Wolf, for instance, appear to have little in common, but both (like the others) are working for a world in which women's contributions will be equally encouraged and rewarded.

Victoria A. Brownworth, "AIDS and Adolescents: Words from the Front" 684

"AIDS and Adolescents" argues that teenagers will become the next wave of victims of the AIDS epidemic. This phenomenon is almost completely preventable, but society's ignorance and complacency will ensure that it occurs.

THE RESPONSIVE READER

1. Brownworth presents teenage AIDS as a mainstream, middle-class problem that strikes "the boy and girl next door." Although most parents prefer to view the disease as belonging to "someone else's kid"—presumed to be a homosexual, runaway, drug user—Brownworth forces a confrontation between such complacency and the true situation. If the article were republished in a mainstream newspaper or magazine or somehow distributed to parents, it would be effective in getting the apathetic majority at least to think about this disease and their teenagers?

2. The story of seventeen-year-old Jarrod is sad and revealing. Critical statistics are that the number of teenagers with AIDS doubles every fourteen months and that in New York and New Jersey AIDS is the leading cause of death for one-to-four-year-old Hispanic children and the leading cause of death for thirteen-to-nineteen-year-old African American and Hispanic women.

3. According to the author, virtually no national or local programs to educate young people or to prevent teenage AIDS exist. This is partly because of the apathy of the majority and partly because the distribution of condoms turns out to be part of attempts at prevention. Parents resist condom distribution by schools as an usurpation of their rights. The director of the Public Health Service is quoted as promoting abstinence and disassociating himself and his organization from condom distribution on the grounds that it encourages "sexual activity." For the experts Brownworth quotes, whether or not teenagers should be sexually active is not the point. They are sexually active, and some are dying as a result.

TALKING, LISTENING, WRITING

4. The deaths of Rock Hudson, Ryan White, Robert Mapplethorpe, Anthony Perkins, and Arthur Ashe and the announcement of his HIV positive status by Magic Johnson should have helped promote recognition and understanding of the disease.

5. Students may report that the dismissal of AIDS as a "gay disease" is slowly beginning to stop?

6. A very personal question.

PROJECTS

7. Endless arguments about needle exchanges or availability of condoms do not bode well for effective attempts at prevention?

Ron Schreiber, "An Alarming New Development" 690

AIDS ultimately does not distinguish between "us" and "them." Only when this point sinks in will a meaningful effort to combat it have a chance.

THE RESPONSIVE READER

1. Pronouns like *they* and *them* allow us to distance ourselves. "They" are the members of the "high-risk groups," and the disease is "their" problem. However, the periodic announcements of heterosexual AIDS are a reminder that the disease will sooner or later reach "all of us." The *we* in the poem are those who are already there, and who will welcome "the rest of us" when the time comes.

2. "They" (a different use of *they*) are trying to kill "us" by not taking the disease seriously (and blaming the victim). Once "they" realize that the entire planet is under siege, it will be time for "them" to "come out / as members of the species." The vast majority of people in the United States (at least at first) thought of AIDS as a disease that struck only homosexuals, drug users, and immigrants from the Caribbean?

TALKING, LISTENING, WRITING

3. Some students may be well informed on the vicissitudes of current research.

PROJECTS

4. The quilt made in tribute to those who have died of AIDS is an example of attempts to commemorate the dead. Larry Kramer, among others, has written a drama on the subject. Memorial occasions and fund-raising efforts by celebrities have been widely publicized.